—MICHAEL PERSHAN—

TEACHING MATH WITH EXAMPLES

JOHN CATT

INDEPENDENT THINKING FOR EDUCATION

First Published 2021

by John Catt Educational Ltd,
15 Riduna Park, Station Road,
Melton, Woodbridge IP12 1QT

Tel: +44 (0) 1394 389850

4600 140th Avenue North,
Suite 180,
Clearwater, FL 33762.
United States

Email: enquiries@johncatt.com
Website: www.johncatt.com

ISBN: 978 1 913622 48 0

Set and designed by John Catt Educational Limited

REVIEWS

"Of all the changes I have made to my teaching since I began engaging with educational research five years ago, my use of worked examples has been the most significant. I now have a structure and routine for worked examples that takes less time, my students enjoy and – most importantly of all – seems to lead to greater understanding. I thought my worked examples had peaked, and finally I could stop thinking about them. Then I read Michael's book, and my world has fallen apart again. What I find fascinating is that Michael has read much the same research as me, and yet we have reached contrasting conclusions. His worked examples look very different to mine, and yet I spent the entire book nodding in agreement.

Michael makes the point that 'some of the dullest teaching on the planet comes courtesy of worked example abusers'. This is so true. If students stare blankly at a teacher's squiggles, nod their heads on cue, don't ask any awkward questions, and then frantically copy down what is on the board into their books, then maths is at risk of becoming the boring, incomprehensible subject many label it as. But the approach Michael presents is interactive, thought-provoking and interesting. There is support scaffolded in for those who initially struggle, and no ceiling imposed for those who grasp the concept more quickly. Above all, the approach has the potential to lay the foundations to enable our students to become the creative, knowledgeable problem solvers we all want them to be.

Rammed full of practical ideas – all of which are beautifully articulated and backed by research – this is a truly wonderful book."

Craig Barton, author of *How I Wish I'd Taught Maths*
and *Reflect, Expect, Check, Explain*

"So often, books about education float high above the work of teaching, with nods to the ways that big ideas and values might look in practice – but without getting much into the muck of the classroom itself. It's such a pleasure as an educator to come across a book that dives deep into instruction, while situating a very specific body of practices (in this case, teaching with worked examples) within a much broader literature on cognitive science and equitable mathematics teaching. Michael Pershan makes a compelling argument for educators to shift their focus from mathematical problem-solving to mathematical understanding – and describes the many ways that exploring and analyzing worked examples can democratize the math classroom, engage learners in rich thinking tasks, and provide targeted, thoughtful scaffolding towards the problem-solving work that math educators (rightfully) value. The book is rich with specific strategies and tools for implementing worked examples – and the theoretical grounding for those ideas, making it a wonderful resource for educators who want something 'they can enact on Monday' and something that strengthens and extends their schema about how math learning (and learning in general) works. As a bonus, it is also a human, funny, and real book about teaching stuff to kids – which is a rarity in itself and makes each chapter a pleasure to read."

Callie Lowenstein, Deans for Impact

"What do you get when you cross a teacher's generosity, a scientist's precision, and a philosopher's dogged pursuit of the truth? Two words: Michael Pershan.

Michael Pershan hears the quiet moments that make education work. Reading this book, I felt he was teaching me how to listen. He takes up the humblest parts of teaching, and he makes them shine. An exemplary book, in every sense."

Ben Orlin, author of *Math With Bad Drawings*

"If you could visit the classroom of a friendly colleague engaging in research-informed practice, while he conversationally whispers in your ear the what, how, and why, it would be something like reading *Teaching Math with Examples*. I can't recommend highly enough this very do-able and high-leverage approach to any math teacher or curriculum developer who wants to level up their task design, or just try out something new."

Kate Nowak, former high school math teacher and currently Vice President of Product Strategy for Illustrative Mathematics

"A good stock of examples, as large as possible, is indispensable for a thorough understanding of any concept, and when I want to learn something new, I make it my first job to build one."

– *Paul Halmos*

To my parents and grandparents.

CONTENTS

Preface: The value of studying examples 11

Introduction: Getting started with examples 13

Chapter 1: How learning from examples works 19

Chapter 2: The case for starting with examples 29

Chapter 3: Routines for learning from examples 39

Chapter 4: Some questions and answers about the routine 53

Chapter 5: Moving from examples to problem solving 61

Chapter 6: Giving worked examples as feedback 77

Chapter 7: Designing worked examples 87

Chapter 8: Teaching proof with examples 99

Afterword: The big ideas of teaching with examples 117

Further reading 119

ACKNOWLEDGEMENTS

Thank you to everyone who read and commented on parts of this book: Rachel Hofmann, Benjamin Blum-Smith, Christian Bokhove, Oliver Lovell, Ryan Gibbons, Courtney Ostaff, Michele Kerr, Benjamin Leis, Kate Nowak, Henri Picciotto, Marian Dingle, Jack Despain, Harry Fletcher-Wood, Max Ray-Riek.

To Alex Sharratt and Mark Combes for capably editing me.

There is no way I could have written this book if Saint Ann's School was not a wonderful place to teach. Thank you to the administration and especially to my colleagues in the math department. Thank you to my students – both at Saint Ann's School and at Bridge to Enter Advanced Mathematics.

The ideas in this book were influenced by so many educators. I especially benefited from those who expressed skepticism about this project at various stages – they pushed me to think more clearly about my teaching. Thank you to you all.

To my wife for encouraging me to take on this book. To my children, for making it nearly impossible to write – I wouldn't have it any other way.

PREFACE: THE VALUE OF STUDYING EXAMPLES

Let's imagine an experiment. We ask two people to try solving a challenging mathematical problem. Along with the problem, both are given a fully worked-out solution to the question, which they can look at whenever they choose. How long will they work on the problem before looking at the solution? Will they look at it at all?

The first person experiments with the problem for a very long time. This person tries an approach, hits a wall, then changes their plan. Then *that* approach doesn't work. So, they try to think out of the box. They reread the question. They review their failed approach and try to understand precisely why it flopped. Then after much struggle, almost by accident they land on a promising strategy. Will it work...? It does! They have done it; the problem is solved. Success!

The second person goes about things differently. They try an approach and it doesn't work. They feel unsure as to how to proceed. After considering their options, the second person decides to look at the solution. They study each line of the solution closely. They puzzle over a difficult step, considering it carefully. Eventually, this second person understands the worked-out solution. They can even explain it all on their own.

Only one of these people was successful in solving the problem. But were they both successful in learning from it?

The question can't be answered because the situation is completely made-up. (For all we know, the first person reflected deeply on their solution and learned a lot from it.) But I'd like us to imagine a likely possibility. That possibility is that even though the first person succeeded in solving the problem, they might not have learned much from the experience. And though the second person failed in one sense, it is entirely possible that they learned something valuable from studying the example with care. If a related challenge were offered again, the second person might now be prepared to persist in solving it. In fact, cognitive science research supports this suggestion (see Chapter 2).

I want my own students to know that *learning* is as important a goal as *problem solving* in mathematics. Failing to solve a problem but learning something from studying the solution is not a failure at all. Forget who came up with the solution for a moment; understanding a new idea is *itself* a creative process, as mathematically impressive as discovering it in the first place. And it's also just as valuable – mathematics needs people who are able to learn challenging ideas with depth.

My favorite articulation of this idea comes from mathematician Bill Thurston. Thurston came across a student of mathematics who, like many of our students, felt inadequate. What can I possibly contribute, this student asked, when there are people out there smarter and better at mathematics than me? Thurston's response:

> Mathematics only exists in a living community of mathematicians that spreads understanding and breathes life into ideas both old and new. **The real satisfaction from mathematics is in learning from others and sharing with others** [emphasis added]. All of us have clear understanding of a few things and murky concepts of many more. There is no way to run out of ideas in need of clarification.[1]

Of course, it is nice when a student solves a problem correctly. From Thurston's perspective, though, correct problem solving is only important because it shows that one has reached "clear understanding." What matters most is whether the student now understands a solution, has made it their own, and is prepared to share it with their peers.

In my view, this is a fundamental shift in perspective that teachers and students need to make. If what we mainly value is problem solving, studying a solution is just giving up. But if we value achieving mathematical understanding, we can see the studying of a solution for what it is: a core mathematical act.

This is something I believe deeply, and it's why I wrote this book.

---

1. Thurnston, B. (2010) "What's a Mathematician To Do?", https://mathoverflow.net/questions/43690/whats-a-mathematician-to-do

INTRODUCTION: GETTING STARTED WITH EXAMPLES

I entered the classroom in 2010, right after I graduated from college. I knew nothing about teaching. Regardless, I was soon teaching algebra and geometry at an all-boys high school in Upper Manhattan. During that first year in the classroom I struggled with each and every aspect of teaching, and I reached out in every direction for help.

I've been reading research since the beginning of my career. At first it was social psychology, where I encountered concepts like "growth mindset" and "intrinsic motivation." Before long I made the move into mathematics education research and getting schooled on problem solving, proof and student misconceptions. More recently, I've been learning about cognitive science and psychology.

I like to think of researchers as colleagues. Each study is an especially well-documented teaching experiment. I learn from reading research in the same way I learn from talking with colleagues. It's not always easy to find colleagues to talk with about these things in person – teaching can be the most solitary activity one does while surrounded by other people. Reading research is a way to connect with other teachers and their experiences. I love it.

Of course, this all takes time. Most teachers have other ways of spending their time besides reading research, and it's not easy to gain access to academic publications. Not to mention the language of academic writing, which can often be daunting. It's no surprise that so few books about research have been written by teachers.

This book is an attempt to explain everything that I have gained from studying research on worked examples. Worked examples are completed solutions that we ask students to study and learn from. (I'll sometimes use "solution" interchangeably with "example.") The work shown is usually correct, though sometimes it can contain errors. Here is a very simple worked example:

$$2x - 4x = 8$$

$$-2x = 8$$
$$\div -2 \qquad \div -2$$
$$\boxed{x = -4}$$

Sometimes they are more complicated, as is this one:

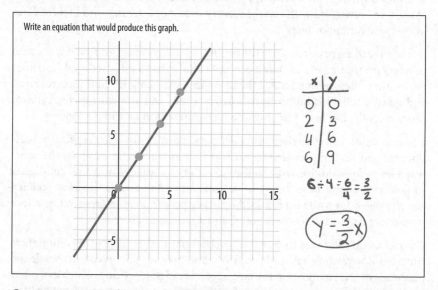

Write an equation that would produce this graph.

Cognitive scientists have amassed evidence in favor of learning from worked examples, with the clearest benefits coming towards the beginning of a learning process.[2] As I read more, I learned that researchers have found other creative ways to use worked examples to help learning. For example, some experiments place two worked examples side-by-side and ask students to learn by comparing them.[3] Other experiments find strong benefits in asking students to explain what's

2. Atkinson, R. K., Derry, S. J., Renkl, A., & Wortham, D. (2000) "Learning from examples: Instructional principles from the worked examples research," *Review of Educational Research*, 70 (2), 181–214.
3. Woodward, J., Beckmann, S., Driscoll, M., Franke, M., Herzig, P., Jitendra, A., Koedinger, K. R., & Ogbuehi, P. (2012) *Improving Mathematical Problem Solving in Grades 4 Through 8*. Institute of Education Sciences.

wrong with mistaken examples.[4] Many teachers consider it easy to design and teach with worked examples – but research suggests this is not the case.[5] Over time, I found ways to incorporate many of these ideas into my classroom work.

Research on worked examples has impacted my teaching in decisive ways, and I'm eager (even a bit nervous) to share what I've learned. This book gives a little window into my teaching. I always learn so much when I visit other teachers' classrooms. I hope you enjoy visiting mine.

The first two chapters of this book are the most theoretical. The first chapter explains the difference between effective and ineffective use of worked examples. The second chapter tries to make the case that there are benefits for starting with examples *early* in the learning process. Even if you intend to challenge your students to solve a challenging, thought-provoking, mathematically rich problem, I think starting with an example can help more students engage productively with it.

From there, the book sticks to the classroom. I have a routine that I use to provide example-based instruction, and I'll share it in Chapter 3. There are some decisions I make in that routine that are worth digging into further – that's the focus of Chapter 4. This covers the beginning of the teaching process.

The end-goal of all teaching is for students to learn to do things independently. Even if we begin with fully guided instruction using examples, we eventually want students to be able to solve problems completely on their own. How do we manage that transition? In Chapter 5 I'll share practice formats that help ease students off examples and into problem solving.

Eventually, teachers want to assess students to see how the learning went, and any assessment leaves us a chance to respond with feedback. I have also found worked examples useful here towards the end of the learning process. In Chapter 6 I will explain how I use examples to give feedback and help students revise.

A huge amount of worked example research is focused on their design. The principles of good example design are useful for creating materials that students can actually learn from. In Chapter 7 I'll share all that I've learned about that.

Finally, Chapter 8 comes from a desire to explore the limits of my pedagogy. I don't want to present a picture of teaching with examples that focuses only on

4. Booth, J. L., Lange, K. E., Koedinger, K. R., & Newton, K. J. (2013) "Using example problems to improve student learning in algebra: Differentiating between correct and incorrect examples," *Learning and Instruction*, 25, 24–34.
5. Ward, M., & Sweller, J. (1990) "Structuring effective worked examples," *Cognition and Instruction*, 7 (1), 1–39.

the easiest cases. I want to test what I've proposed in the first seven chapters against one of the most challenging topics that I teach: geometric proof. In this last chapter, I'll explain how the same principles at the heart of my teaching can be applied to proof, though some details must change.

As an expression of my love of research, I've ended the book with a "Further Reading" section. If you're ready to dive deeper into the world of journal articles and literature reviews, this section is for you.

PREVIEW OF WHAT'S TO COME

This book is written for math teachers, and I know that every teacher is busy. Before moving into the heart of the book, I'd like to begin by providing the quickest, simplest ways to begin teaching with examples.

Every math teacher asks their students to practice solving problems. A well-done worksheet gives students a variety of problems that systematically increase in complexity. Many worksheets, however, are far too repetitive. If a student can solve one problem, what do they gain from solving another similar one? If a student can't solve the first, why make them do it again and again?

One of the first and most practical suggestions to come out of worked example research involves transforming the repetitive form that worksheet practice takes.[6] It's not hard at all to incorporate these recommendations into your work. To do it, take your worksheet of somewhat repetitive practice and pick a few problems to solve. Maybe solve the first but leave the second for students to try. (This creates what's called an "example-problem pair.") If the problems are complex, consider solving most of a problem while leaving a step for students to complete. If students are ready for it, consider making a mistake in your solution and asking students to explain the error.

---

6. Sweller, J., & Cooper, G. A. (1985) "The use of worked examples as a substitute for problem solving in learning algebra," *Cognition and Instruction*, 2 (1), 59–89.

Your worksheet, by the end, might look like this:

Study this:	Solve this:
$37 = -3 + 5(x + 6)$	$-13 = 5(1 + 4m) - 2m$
$37 = -3 + 5x + 30$	
$37 = 27 + 5x$	
$10 = 5x$	
$x = 2$	
Complete the problem:	Explain why this solution is incorrect:
$4(-x + 4) = 12$	$-2 = -(n - 8)$
$-4x + 16 = 12$	$-2 = -n - 8$
$-4x = -4$	$6 = -n$
	$n = -6$

This is already a great way to begin.

Where do we go from here? Some teachers might tell you that there's little to say about teaching with examples – after all, everyone uses them. But here are just some of the questions we might ask about teaching with worked examples:

- How do we introduce an example?
- What do we ask students to do when studying a solution?
- Should a solution be presented all at once or revealed step by step?
- After we study an example, what comes next?
- Does it matter if the solution is presented as if from a fictional student, a real student in class, or from the teacher?
- How do we help students move from understanding someone else's idea towards using it on their own to solve problems?
- How do we write a solution in a clear way, that students can learn from?
- When is a good time to offer a worked example? When is it better to let students try a problem?
- Are worked examples more useful for some mathematical content than others?

This book will answer all these questions. In some cases, research offers answers. That research has been useful to me, and I'll show how it informed my teaching. Other questions represent gaps in the research literature, and I'll share the solutions I've arrived at through experience and trial-and-error – my own process of classroom problem solving.

Welcome to the world of teaching with examples!

CHAPTER 1: HOW LEARNING FROM EXAMPLES WORKS

Some of the dullest teaching on the planet comes courtesy of worked example abusers. These are the math classes that consist of a steady march of definitions, explanations and examples, one after the next. Practice (and learning) happen out of the classroom hours later, while students work on their homework. With few exceptions, we've all had these kinds of teachers at one point or another. Many of us, at times, have *been* this kind of teacher.

This is not good teaching. Some students will learn from examples presented in this way, but not nearly enough. Nevertheless, a large body of research shows "an advantage for learning and transfer if people study worked examples," as research psychologist Bethany Rittle-Johnson puts it.[7] Of course, this research doesn't certify *every* possible use of worked examples in the classroom, and any instructional method can be misused. This raises the question: what's the difference between worked examples done well and done poorly?

Rittle-Johnson herself offers an answer to this question. It seems simple, but the point is lost too often: what matters for learning is what is going on inside a student's head. Whether one is teaching with a worked example or asking students to make their own discoveries, learning can only happen when careful thinking occurs. Rittle-Johnson writes:

> The potential benefits of discovery learning may be due to **actively engaging the learner in manipulating, linking, and evaluating information** – in other words, self-explanation – rather than the discovery of the procedure itself. Successful uses of direct instruction may emerge when learners are **engaged in active cognitive processes** like self-explanation [emphasis added].[8]

Teaching only works when it provokes this sort of active, deeper thought: "manipulating, linking, and evaluating information." Performing a series of worked examples while students drool into their notebooks doesn't meet this

---

7. Rittle-Johnson, B. (2006) "Promoting transfer: Effects of self-explanation and direct instruction," *Child Development*, 77 (1), 1–15.
8. Ibid.

standard. Neither does discovering a solution if students discover it by guessing. Either approach can, and often does, fail to produce learning. Educational techniques are not magic. If they don't provoke thinking, they don't work. (Cognitive scientist Daniel Willingham puts it like this: "memory is the residue of thought.")[9]

This is a book about worked examples, so you won't be surprised to hear that I find the research supporting them to be compelling. But it's important to take Rittle-Johnson's point to heart. Students do not learn *from* a worked example; students learn when they think actively and deeply about a worked example. To make the case for teaching with them, we need to explain what active and deep engagement with them looks like.

There are two major ways that students can fail to learn from a worked example:

- Students don't think actively and deeply about the worked-out solution.
- Students aren't ready to understand the problem and its worked-out solution.

As we'll see, there are ways of designing activities that avoid these pitfalls.

ANALYZE, EXPLAIN AND APPLY: THINKING DEEPLY ABOUT EXAMPLES

At first, I was skeptical of research supporting learning from worked examples. I assumed that research would recommend methods I knew not to be effective – a teacher standing at the board for long periods of time, working out the solutions to problems step by painful step, pausing every so often to ask the class a question. ("And why do we subtract three from both sides? Anybody? Somebody?") This is, after all, the most common mode of math instruction that students experience in the United States.[10] If *that's* what research was recommending, some enormous mistake must have been made.

The Algebra by Example project helped change my mind.[11] This project represents the fruit of a partnership between a team of researchers and a school district to help their students learn algebra. The researchers used research literature to create a collection of worked examples. They then tested the examples in the classroom while performing an experiment that showed the

9. Willingham, D. T. (2008) "What will improve a student's memory," *American Educator*, 32 (4), 17–25.

10. Stigler, J. W., Gonzales, P., Kawanaka, T., Knoll, S., & Serrano, A. (1999) "The TIMSS videotape classroom study: Methods and findings from an exploratory research project on eighth-grade mathematics instruction in Germany, Japan, and the United States," *Education Statistics Quarterly*, 1 (2), 109–112.

11. Algebra by Example (SERP Institute): https://www.serpinstitute.org/algebra-by-example

materials actually worked as intended.[12] After testing, they posted the materials for free online so that any teacher could use them. They've since created and tested materials for elementary school students ("Math by Example") and are currently working on middle-school mathematics.[13] This seemed to me a best-case scenario for research that is relevant to the needs of classroom teachers.

Once I saw their materials, it became clear that I had completely misunderstood what the research recommended. I thought research called on teachers to simply present worked examples without worrying about student engagement. What I saw instead were activities that guided students towards deep thinking. A complete mathematical strategy was presented through the worked example, and students were prompted to explain why it worked. Then they were tasked with using the strategy to solve a related problem on their own. This was an active and interesting set of activities – my students would love them.

The Algebra by Example materials always ask students to do three things:

1. **Analyze** a solution.
2. **Explain** why it works.
3. **Apply** it to a new problem.

You can see these three steps at play in any of their materials. Here is an example activity of my own in the Algebra by Example style:

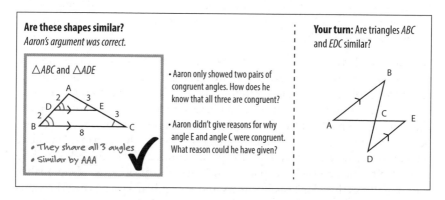

---

12. Booth, J. L., Oyer, M. H., Paré-Blagoev, E. J., Elliot, A. J., Barbieri, C., Augustine, A., & Koedinger, K. R. (2015) "Learning algebra by example in real-world classrooms," *Journal of Research on Educational Effectiveness*, 8 (4), 530–551.
13. Math by Example (SERP Institute): https://www.serpinstitute.org/math-by-example

This is "direct instruction" by any definition – students are tasked with learning from a worked-out solution presented by the teacher. But it doesn't fit the stereotype of boring, passive learning. Students are given something mathematically valuable and asked to think about it.

In the **analyze** stage, students begin by carefully reading a worked-out solution – an activity that puts students in direct contact with new and challenging mathematical ideas. As students closely analyze the procedure, they may ask: *Does this make sense? Do I understand what the solution did? Why did it do this? Could I do this on my own?* Students learn from asking and answering these questions, engaging in what Rittle-Johnson and other researchers call "self-explanation."

Not always, though. Stretching back to nearly the beginning of worked examples research is an awareness that not all students ask themselves these probing questions. This research was pioneered by Michelene T. H. Chi, who also suggested that the propensity to self-explain is responsible for some of the differences between stronger and weaker students.[14] In her studies, students who successfully learned from worked examples were more likely to explain the examples to themselves as they read them. Other students studied the examples superficially, reading each line but failing to engage in self-explanation. These students were less likely to learn from the examples, and often failed to apply the strategies they studied to new problems. Superficial engagement is perhaps the most common obstacle in the way of learning from a worked example. It's what happens in passive, lecture-heavy classrooms across the planet: students listen, but they aren't thinking.

A solution to this problem is straightforward: after reading the example, prompt students to **explain** it themselves. Calling on students to explain represents the second stage of the Algebra by Example activities. It serves to draw attention to aspects of a solution that students might have skimmed over. If artfully chosen, these prompts direct students to consider ideas in the solution they might not have even realized they didn't understand. Booth writes that this may "facilitate integration of new information with prior knowledge and force learners to make their new knowledge explicit."[15] In other words, when students realize there are things they don't easily understand, it highlights what is new. Prompts are a sort of "safety net" for students who read the solution superficially at first.

14. Chi, M. T., Bassok, M., Lewis, M. W., Reimann, P., & Glaser, R. (1989) "Self-explanations: How students study and use examples in learning to solve problems," *Cognitive Science*, 13 (2), 145–182.

15. Booth, J. L., Oyer, M. H., Paré-Blagoev, E. J., Elliot, A. J., Barbieri, C., Augustine, A., & Koedinger, K. R. (2015) "Learning algebra by example in real-world classrooms," *Journal of Research on Educational Effectiveness*, 8 (4), 530–551.

When students realize they can't explain something, they go back to step one and analyze the example with more zest.

In the third stage, students are asked to **apply** what they know to a new problem. If the problem has been chosen well, this pushes students to form generalizations – they compare their solution to this problem to the solution they just read. Solving the problem sends many students right back into opportunities for self-explanation: *Does the solution I just studied work here? Did I really understand the solution? Which parts of the solution will look different, and which will remain the same?* The teacher can prompt even more of this reflection during a follow-up discussion.

SELF-EXPLANATION RESEARCH

Research on self-explanation has blossomed in the years since Chi's groundbreaking work. There are now many, many studies exploring how to effectively prompt students to self-explain. In brief, here are some of the most important lessons of self-explanation research taken from reviews by Renkl & Eitel (2019)[16] and Rittle-Johnson et al. (2017):[17]

- Like learning from examples in general, the greatest benefits of self-explanation come towards the beginning of the learning process. Once students have gone beyond the "initial acquisition" phase, self-explanation offers little benefit and can distract from other beneficial activities (Renkl & Eitel, 2019).
- "Self-explanation" can refer to a variety of activities. When it comes to learning mathematics, the sort of self-explanation that is most often beneficial is that which connects particular examples to general principles that can be applied to other problems (Renkl & Eitel, 2019).
- Students often do not know what good "self-explanation" looks like. Studies find benefits to explicitly showing students what a good self-explanation looks like by analyzing an example of an excellent explanation or modeling it for the class (Rittle-Johnson et al. 2017).

16. Renkl, A., & Eitel, A. (2019) "Self-explaining: Learning about principles and their application," in J. Dunlosky & K. Rawson (eds.), *Cambridge Handbook of Cognition and Education*, 528–549.
17. Rittle-Johnson, B., Loehr, A. M., & Durkin, K. (2017) "Promoting self-explanation to improve mathematics learning: A meta-analysis and instructional design principles," *ZDM*, 49 (4), 599–611.

- Other studies provide very structured prompts for self-explanation by asking students to choose between two explanations or to fill in the blanks to complete an otherwise excellent explanation (Renkl & Eitel 2019, Rittle-Johnson et al. 2017).

It seems to me that the surest way to bring this research into classroom practice is to teach students what good mathematical explanation looks like. Whenever possible, encourage students to include a "because" in their answers. Push students to connect particular details with general rules or principles in their explanations. We should model this in our own explanations ("4/8 is equal to 1/2 because in both the denominator is twice the numerator"). Classrooms that are brimming with good explanations will help support student self-explanation.

It should be clear that asking students to **analyze**, **explain** and then **apply** worked examples to new problems is *not* the passive direct instruction that is often subjected to critiques in educational debates. This is something altogether different – an active, engaged direct instruction. It should hardly seem surprising that this form of teaching would benefit students.

NOTICE AND REMEMBER: PREPARING TO LEARN FROM AN EXAMPLE

Even if we could guarantee that students analyzed every example with care – making sure they engaged in deep self-explanation – there would be times that learning would fail. That's because frequently students will not be prepared to learn from the example.

The research concerning this question is somewhat confusing, with claims and counterclaims tossed back and forth. Some researchers have argued that working on the problem *before* studying a worked example is important for learning. Manu Kapur, for instance, has argued that this has benefits even if the student fails to correctly solve the problem – he calls this "productive failure."[18] Slava Kalyuga and Anne-Marie Singh suggest that solving a problem before an example might be useful for helping a student understand what a problem is even asking and what its solution may look like.[19] Likewise, Schwartz and

---

18. Kapur, M. (2008) "Productive failure," *Cognition and Instruction*, 26 (3), 379–424.
19. Kalyuga, S., & Singh, A. M. (2016) "Rethinking the boundaries of cognitive load theory in complex learning," *Educational Psychology Review*, 28 (4), 831–852.

Martin suggest that inventing an inefficient procedure prepares students to more quickly and effectively learn from examples and explanations.[20]

Meanwhile, other researchers have performed experiments showing advantages to example-first teaching,[21] and still others have found no differences between example–problem and problem–example approaches.[22] It's all very confusing, and researchers are currently trying to design studies that could explain these conflicting results.

Just as we did before, to make sense of this debate I think it's helpful to dig deeper. There are at least two mental processes that are crucial prerequisites for learning from a solution:

- Students must **notice** everything in the problem that will be involved in its solution.
- Students must **remember** previous knowledge and strategies that are taken for granted in the solution.

Consider, for instance, this worked example for finding the length of a trapezoid base, given its area and other lengths. It's a lot to take in all at once! Noticing and remembering certain information is a prerequisite for learning from the solution:

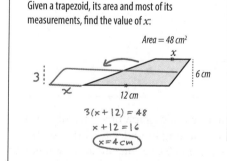

Given a trapezoid, its area and most of its measurements, find the value of x:

$Area = 48 \, cm^2$

$3(x + 12) = 48$

$x + 12 = 16$

$x = 4 \, cm$

Things to notice:
- Shape is a trapezoid
- Height of 6 cm, bottom base 12 cm
- Area of 48 cm²
- Top base is labeled x

Things to remember:
- How to solve $3(x + 12) = 48$
- How to find the area of a parallelogram

20. Schwartz, D. L., & Martin, T. (2004) "Inventing to prepare for future learning: The hidden efficiency of encouraging original student production in statistics instruction," *Cognition and Instruction*, 22 (2), 129–184.

21. Ashman, G., Kalyuga, S., & Sweller, J. (2020) "Problem-solving or explicit instruction: Which should go first when element interactivity is high?," *Educational Psychology Review*, 32 (1), 229–247.

22. Likourezos, V., & Kalyuga, S. (2017) "Instruction-first and problem-solving-first approaches: Alternative pathways to learning complex tasks," *Instructional Science*, 45 (2), 195–219.

If students don't notice everything about the problem or if they don't remember necessary material, they aren't likely to gain much from analyzing a solution.

I often precede a worked example with a short problem to solve. These problems tend to be brief, as I want my students to save their energy for working through a solution. When they work, I think it's because they help my students notice and remember information crucial for the example.

Suppose, for instance, that I'm teaching a class to write linear equations from graphs of lines. They'll need to **remember** how to find the slope of that line for the solution to make any sense. They've studied this already, of course, but I would like to remind them. I'll give them a problem before the example:

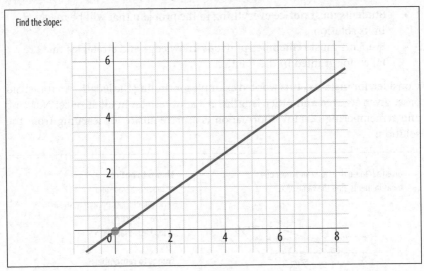

There is also a ton of information contained in a graph of a line, all of which I would like students to **notice** before attempting to understand the solution. I might share that same diagram and say, "I'd like everyone to notice something about this diagram – the more specific, the better." I'd then ask students to share what they see. They might say any of the following:

- There is a line.
- The numbers go by 2.
- The line passes through 6 and 4. ("It's (6, 4)," I'll remind them.)
- It also passes through (0, 0).

Each of these observations will be useful when I present an example showing how to find the equation of a line.

This is how I make sense of the narrower debate about whether solving problems enhances learning from examples. Students need help noticing and remembering details that will appear in the solution; problems can help students do this. There are ways to do this without asking students to solve problems, but I find it useful to launch class with a brief warm-up problem anyway. I might as well use it to support their upcoming learning.

I also suspect that these warm-up problems provide a motivational boost to students as they head into a worked example. It shows them that class is going to be focused on extending that which they already know and understand. A quick problem allows me to clearly articulate the purpose of the day's class – we've already studied this, but today we're taking it further. I have rarely experienced issues motivating students to study worked examples compared to other classroom activities. I attribute this to my use of notice/remember problems, along with the analyze/explain/apply structure I have adopted for teaching with examples.

Worked examples don't always work, but done well they can be powerful tools for learning. The key is to get students thinking about the new mathematics in as direct a way as possible – that means they can learn from **analyzing** a solution. To make sure that analysis has been careful, we encourage students to **explain** crucial aspects of the solution. To help students generalize the solution (and to further ensure they're thinking carefully), we can ask them to **apply** it to a new problem.

To learn from a solution, students need to **notice** crucial aspects of the problem. They also need to **remember** some things they have already learned. A problem that comes before an example can help students notice and remember this information, and so enhances their learning from the example.

Is this the only way to learn? Is it the only technique you need for learning math? Of course not. But worked examples don't deserve to be seen as a tool of passive, boring instruction. What research on worked examples actually points to is a set of learning activities that provoke lively, active thinking in our students. Using these techniques, we put our students in direct contact with some new and interesting ideas.

But when is a good time to use these examples in our teaching? When is it better to give students problems to solve on their own? That's the subject of the next chapter.

IN SHORT

- Cognitive science and experimental psychology have produced evidence in support of learning from worked examples. To get the full benefits, however, students need to be prompted to engage deeply with the examples.
- Asking students to **analyze** a solution, **explain** important details, and **apply** the solution to a new problem can help students learn from examples.
- At times, it may be useful to precede an example with a short problem that helps students **notice** and **remember** information that will be necessary for understanding the worked example.

CHAPTER 2: THE CASE FOR STARTING WITH EXAMPLES

When is it best to study an example: early or late?

Many math educators are in favor of studying examples relatively late in the game. To give an example of this perspective, consider how the Connected Mathematics Project (a curriculum for Grades 6–8) describes their lesson design:

> Problem-centered teaching and learning opens the mathematics classroom to exploring, conjecturing, reasoning, and communicating... The CMP teacher materials are organized around an instructional model that supports this kind of "inquiry-based" teaching. This model is very different from the "transmission" or "direct instruction" model, in which teachers tell students facts and demonstrate procedures and then students memorize the facts and practice the procedures. The CMP model looks at instruction in three phases: launching, exploring, and summarizing.[23]

The lessons begin with a "launch," whose purpose is to help students understand and work on the upcoming problem. During the "explore" phase students are given a problem and asked to solve it, using their own ideas. It's only at the end of the lesson during the "summary" when teachers help students "reach the mathematical goals of the problem." This lesson structure is mirrored in the structure of the units – they begin with problem solving and only aim for everyone to attain the target skill later in the unit. Worked examples, if they enter this picture at all, come late.

Worked examples research has a different perspective. Cognitive scientists and psychologists recommend that worked examples come early, towards the beginning of learning something new: "learning from worked examples is of major importance in **initial stage**s of cognitive skills acquisition," is how Atkinson et al. summarize the evidence.[24]

---

23. Connected Mathematics Project, "Philosophy": https://connectedmath.msu.edu/curriculum-design/philosophy/
24. Atkinson, R. K., Derry, S. J., Renkl, A., & Wortham, D. (2000) "Learning from examples: Instructional principles from the worked examples research," *Review of Educational Research*, 70 (2), 181–214.

This same literature describes the importance of moving to problem solving as students gain more expertise. This is sometimes described as an "expertise reversal effect".[25] As students gain knowledge, the same experiments that show advantages to worked examples begin to show advantages for solving practice problems. "During these stages," Renkl and Atkinson write, "it is important that the learners actually solve problems as opposed to studying examples."[26]

Now, this is a book about worked examples – I haven't signed up to discuss the full merits and drawbacks of different curricular approaches. But I don't want to ignore the "examples later" perspective that many in math education stand by. It's worth explaining why I think that everyone – even users of curricula like CMP – should consider an "examples early" approach.

In what follows I'll make the case for starting with examples, even if you use a curriculum focused on learning from problem solving. This argument comes in two parts:

- First, the way we learn from solving problems is the same way we learn from studying examples – by thinking actively and deeply about the solution. As a result, the most direct path to learning in many situations is to analyze a problem *along* with its solution.
- Starting with an example doesn't take away the opportunity for students to creatively engage with a mathematics problem; it expands access to that engagement, reducing the number of students who are unproductively stuck on the task.

Taken together, this chapter will argue that there's nothing to lose and much to gain from starting with examples early, no matter your educational philosophy.

LEARNING FROM EXAMPLES AND PROBLEM SOLVING

To understand the case for starting with examples, we need to first understand how it is that people learn from solving a problem.

In the 1950s, experimental psychology in the United States was dominated by behaviorism. The behaviorists were intensely skeptical of the unobservable – you can't see a thought! – and therefore eliminated the inner mental world from their research. All sorts of concepts that are now widely used were considered too "mentalistic" for serious research: beliefs, strategies, working memory,

25. Kalyuga, S. (2007) "Expertise reversal effect and its implications for learner-tailored instruction," *Educational Psychology Review*, 19 (4), 509–539.
26. Renkl, A., & Atkinson, R. K. (2003) "Structuring the transition from example study to problem solving in cognitive skill acquisition: A cognitive load perspective," *Educational Psychologist*, 38 (1), 15–22.

concepts, and so on. If you can't directly see it, then it wasn't real enough for the behaviorists.

Cognitive science began as a movement reacting against the behaviorist orthodoxy. They amassed findings that were difficult to explain only in terms of behavior – things that pointed to an inner mental life that could be scientifically studied. Soon, cognitive scientists were studying a wide variety of subjects. One of these subjects was learning from problem solving.[27]

Cognitive scientists knew that after correctly solving a problem, people often were able to better solve future problems. Clearly, learning could happen. But how? As one widely cited review puts it, "students learn by solving problems and reflecting on their experiences".[28] Mathematician George Pólya agrees in his book *How To Solve It*:

> Even fairly good students, when they have obtained the solution of the problem and written down neatly the argument, shut their books and look for something else. Doing so, they miss an important and instructive phase of the work. By looking back at the completed solution, by reconsidering and reexamining the result and the path that led to it, they could consolidate their knowledge and develop their ability to solve problems.[29]

In other words, students don't primarily gain knowledge from solving the problem – they learn from thinking about the solution.

Does this sound familiar? Isn't this precisely how students learn from worked examples? If so, could the learning benefits that come from solving a problem be gained from skipping ahead to studying its solution?

John Sweller was one of the first cognitive scientists to study this. Over the course of many experiments, he found support for a "worked example effect" – advantages to devoting time to studying a solution versus successfully solving a problem.[30] The advantages of learning from a worked example come in two ways. First, the worked example isolates the new idea and makes sure that students

---

27. Part of this interest came from the desire to create artificial intelligence, a field that was emerging from computer science and cognitive science at this time. See the Further Reading section for more on the early history of cognitive science.

28. Hmelo-Silver, C. E. (2004) "Problem-based learning: What and how do students learn?," *Educational Psychology Review*, 16 (3), 235–266.

29. Pólya, G. (2004) *How to solve it: A new aspect of mathematical method* (Vol. 85). Princeton University Press.

30. Sweller, J. (2016) "Story of a research program," *Education Review*, 23.

spend time thinking about it. Even when students successfully solve a problem they usually use their existing strategies, and therefore spend relatively less time studying the new, more powerful approach. In one study, Sweller et al. created a number puzzle that challenged students to use "multiply by 3" or "subtract 69" to turn a start number to a target.[31] Most students never discovered that the problems could all be solved by alternating multiplication and subtraction; they simply did whatever would make their number closer to the target.

I have seen this play out many times in the classroom, especially with young students. You ask them to solve 21 minus 3 using a mental strategy, but you come around to their paper and see them drawing 21 lines on their page and crossing out 3 of them. Of course, the teacher can then ask the student to consider a different strategy during a looking back, reflective phase of a lesson. Worked examples show advantages because it puts this reflective phase at the start of learning, not the end.

A second reason for the "worked example effect" has to do with cognitive capacities. These capacities are things like attention (our ability to focus on information) or working memory (our capacity to temporarily hold on to information). Solving an unfamiliar problem forces our attention to flit between many different places. There is a lot to notice – not all of which is useful for learning a new mathematical idea. Putting together a solution also requires holding a lot of potentially useful information in one's head, which taxes working memory. Both attention and working memory are limited resources. If our resources are spent solving the problem, there is little left in the tank to devote towards learning. This insight is central to John Sweller's "cognitive load theory," which describes how to design learning with these cognitive limits in mind.[32]

In sum, it's not that students can't learn from solving problems. Mathematicians, math educators and cognitive scientists all agree that they can, *if* they reflect back on their solutions and analyze them. It's this analysis process that is necessary for learning. Without it, students may never even consider the new, more powerful strategy the teacher would like to help the class learn. But if analyzing a solution is the key to learning from problem solving, it is also possible to learn from studying the solutions themselves, i.e. worked examples. If you could skip ahead to directly studying an example, you'd expect learning to happen more quickly and reliably – as long as students understand the solution and really think deeply about it. This is precisely what research finds.

---

31. Sweller, J., Mawer, R. F., & Howe, W. (1982) "Consequences of history-cued and means-end strategies in problem solving," *The American Journal of Psychology*, 455–483.
32. For more on cognitive load theory, see the Further Reading section.

What comes next is practice (see Chapter 5 for more on that), which will inevitably involve problem solving. The choice is not between solving a problem and studying its solution; it's about *when* you choose to prioritize either of these things, and research suggests there are benefits of studying examples in the early stages of learning.

EXAMPLES AND CREATIVE ENGAGEMENT

For many math educators, all this about the benefits of examples is beside the point. "True," they'd say, "if my only goal were to teach content then worked examples would be the way to go. But that's not why I teach with problems. I use problems because I want my students to experience the mathematical process in its fullest expression." The CMP curriculum has "exploring, conjecturing, reasoning, and communicating" about mathematics as core goals. You can't do that with a worked example, they'd argue.[33]

Of course, these educators also want to teach students how to solve problems. They might use worked examples *later*, after students have had a chance to explore, conjecture, reason and communicate about some problem. I also value these things, and for a few years, this was how I primarily approached my own classroom work.

At the start of class I would assign a problem. Students got chances to be creative and collaborate on new and challenging pieces of mathematics. Some students reached a solution by the end of class; others did not. Those who did would have a chance to share, even if their approaches weren't new or particularly efficient. I would record their solutions clearly on the board. The class would, essentially, treat each of their peer's approaches as a worked-out solution to learn from. (Or, alternatively, I would present an approach that no one had thought of yet.) Because students had put so much effort into the problem, I thought they would be eager to learn from their classmates' solutions. They would analyze them with enthusiasm, explain why they worked, and then apply those ideas in their own problem solving.

This sounds so nice, but in practice it's not what I saw. As time went on, I grew dissatisfied by each stage of this routine. I also came to believe that starting

---

33. I'm not so sure that you can't. We've already seen that research suggests that students explain and analyze solutions – isn't that reasoning and communicating? And if we start with a short problem that helps students notice and remember information that is relevant to the example, doesn't that count as exploring and conjecturing? Admittedly, an "examples early" approach would spend relatively little time on this conjecturing/exploring; for CMP, it's the whole point of the lesson. In any event, I think studying examples should be considered just as mathematical as reasoning, as I argued in the Preface.

with a worked example *before* asking students to engage in this sort of problem solving could make things better.

When students are given challenging opportunities, they are also necessarily given a chance to grow frustrated and feel as if they've failed. To manage this, I would come to class prepared with hints and probing questions for students who felt stuck. When students called for help or when I saw their efforts flagging, I would prompt them with my hints or questions. But while I was helping one student, many others were waiting for my attention. And if students didn't understand the hint, it would often take a long time to present this new idea to them. Eventually I asked myself: how could I do this more effectively?

My answer: I could teach those hints and suggestions to the entire class before work on the problem began. I'd present a worked example showing a strategy *before* sharing a challenging problem.

For instance, while teaching a problem-solving class at a math enrichment camp I found a problem I knew my students would find challenging: *"One thermos of hot chocolate uses 2/3 cup of cocoa powder. How many thermoses can Nelli make with 3 cups of cocoa powder?"*

The hint that I wanted to give many of my students if (really, when) they got stuck on it was to draw a diagram representing the situation. But I could already imagine the problems my students would have with that hint. What sort of diagram? Which parts should we represent? What does it look like?

To make sure students would know what sort of diagram I meant, I started class with a worked example showing exactly what I was imagining:

Example:

3/4 of a can of paint is enough to paint 1 wall.
How many walls could you paint with 2 cans of paint?

Marcia's solution:

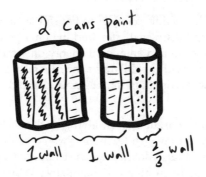

Questions:

- Why did she split the cans of paint into quarters?
- How did she know that two quarters of paint would cover two thirds of a wall?

This didn't eliminate the challenge for my students when they turned to the problems – it democratized it, helping more students join in on the challenge.

I had similar concerns about who got to share solutions. I used to work very, very hard to make sure that it was not only "those kids" who shared ideas at the end of problem solving. I'd circle the room and actively seek out interesting ideas from students – especially quieter students, or those who saw themselves as bad at math. I'd help them refine their ideas, and then ask if I could call on them to share those ideas during the discussion. I would give them time to shine.

Still, it was an uphill battle. At the end of the day, I was asking students to work on a problem no one had taught them how to do before; it is no surprise that some students consistently had more success at this than others. And it also won't surprise any teacher that these tasks were most frustrating for the students who I most wanted to feel successful – those children who were convinced they were bad at math, or who felt socially isolated from the class for other reasons.[34]

---

34. Another concern I had: students would sometimes be reluctant to move away from inefficient ideas that they shared in front of the class. After all, that was their time to shine! They loved their approach. Praising students for an inefficient approach has a place, but I worried that I was making it harder for them to adopt more efficient strategies.

Starting with examples gives me a chance to level the playing field. When I present a strategy early, it helps narrow the knowledge gaps between my students before the challenge begins. Since explanation is a key part of how I teach with examples (Chapter 1), it also gives far more students the chance to share their explanations at the very start of class.

One last concern with pushing examples to the end of class: I often found that students were tired and distracted after working on a problem. They had just expended so much mental and emotional energy on searching for a solution. Solving problems can be either exhilarating or frustrating – sometimes both at once! These are not ideal conditions for beginning to study something new and perhaps challenging.

None of this is meant to argue against giving students challenging problems to solve on their own. In my own teaching, I would call this kind of problem solving a "sometimes" thing. I do this because I value these things, and because they can sometimes be interesting and energizing. While it's hardly the only thing I care about, I do care about students leaving my class with an accurate picture of what mathematics is like as a discipline, and mathematics involves thinking hard about interesting problems. There's a place for that in math class.

How much time a class chooses to spend on these sorts of challenges will depend on so many factors. How comfortable are the students with being pushed in this way? Do students seem bored with the regular learning routine? (Variety is the spice of teaching.) What are the expectations of the school and the math department? What are the expectations of students' caregivers? Not least of all, are my students meeting the expectations of the course? Are they ready for more? There is no one-size-fits-all prescription for problem solving.

Whatever amount of challenging, creative problem solving you're asking students to do, it can help to precede it with worked examples. If teachers are prepared to offer hints and suggestions to students when they are stuck on a problem, they should be prepared to make sure every student is prepared to really understand them.

What I have learned to do is pick the most essential hint and capture it in a worked example. I present it to the entire class early in the lesson or unit, and I refer back to it when students are stuck. "Do you remember the diagram in that solution we studied?" I'll say to a student who asks for help. "You could do something like that here." Very often, that helps.

PROBLEM-SOLVING STRATEGIES

Many mathematics teachers encourage their students to employ high-level strategies while working on challenging mathematics, like "Draw a Picture" or "Solve a Simpler Case."

Many of these strategies are credited to mathematician George Pólya, author of *How to Solve It*. But, as mathematics education researcher Alan Schoenfeld has written, "Pólya's characterizations did not provide the amount of detail that would enable people who were not already familiar with the strategies to be able to implement them."[35]

Worked examples can make this more effective. Find another problem that exemplifies the strategy you'd like students to learn. Study and identify the strategy you'd like students to use on the challenge with them *before* they attempt the challenge. If students aren't able to apply the strategy to the new challenge, that may be a warning sign: the challenge is going to be too difficult.

Whether you're trying to teach mathematical skills or give students a chance to engage in creative mathematics, I see advantages for starting with worked examples. A key insight is that people learn from examples and problems in the exact same way – from thinking deeply about the solutions. Whether that comes before or after trying the problem doesn't matter very much. Why not directly focus on the solution, then?

One reason is because math class can be about more than just learning skills. It can be a chance for students to engage in all sorts of mathematical activities that are connected to the discipline. For some people, math class is all about giving students a chance to engage in rich problem solving. That's not my orientation (see the Preface), but I do see value in sometimes giving students a juicy mathematical problem to work on. If for no other reason, just because it can be a lot of fun.

Making sure the problem actually is fun for everyone is not easy on a teacher, though. What I've found is that starting with a worked example can help. It helps push some students who would be struggling unproductively into a more productive place. An example can present a strategy that the teacher can prompt students with when they're feeling stuck. And discussing an example gives more students a chance to share their explanations – after all, this example doesn't

35. Schoenfeld, A. H. (1992) "Learning to think mathematically: Problem solving, metacognition, and sense making in mathematics," in Grouws, D. A. (ed.) *Handbook of Research on Mathematics Teaching and Learning*. Macmillan.

"belong" to any student in the class. It's nobody's strategy, until we study it and make it our own.

IN SHORT

- Students learn from problem solving when they reflect deeply on a solution. **Worked examples *also* allow students to reflect on a solution**, without first requiring them to solve it.
- There are creative mathematical practices that students can only engage in through challenging problem solving, such as conjecturing and exploring. **Challenging mathematical activities sometimes leave students feeling unproductively stuck.**
- To help students who would be unproductively stuck on a challenging task, **study a worked example before launching a classroom challenge**. The worked example can contain a useful strategy that the teacher can refer back to when students ask for help during the challenge.

CHAPTER 3: ROUTINES FOR LEARNING FROM EXAMPLES

I read a lot of research on education, at least for a classroom teacher. I usually have a paper or two printed out in my backpack that I'm looking forward to reading and thinking about. Occasionally, a teacher friend who knows about this habit will name some educational practice and ask me whether there's research for it. I never know exactly what to say. Often it turns out they're looking for research to help settle a disagreement with parents or school administration. They want evidence that props up their case – that's a use of research I don't really believe in.

Without getting bogged down in semantics, I think there is a difference between **evidence-based** teaching and **evidence-informed** teaching. The main difference is that the first is mostly impossible and the second is hard but valuable. "Classrooms are just too complicated for research ever to tell teachers what to do," researcher and educator Dylan Wiliam says, and I agree.[36] Unless your argument is taking place on terms that are a few steps removed from actual classrooms, research usually can't definitively settle it. Teaching can't really be *based* on research.

I'd define "evidence-informed teaching" as however it is you teach when you understand the research evidence. I don't believe teaching can ever be evidence-based, but I think it would be terrific if teaching became more informed by evidence. As Wiliam says, this wouldn't lead to a total convergence in techniques. We teachers all have different abilities and dispositions, and many of us even have different classrooms goals. We'll never all teach the same, and that's OK by me.

Think of teaching as a landscape and research as the map. Not every hiker will take the same route, and we aren't all trying to get to the same place. But a good, accurate map is useful to everybody.

Taking that analogy one step further: let me show you one of my favorite paths through the territory – a routine for learning from worked examples. It is informed by research, but it is not the only way to take the principles of worked

---

36. Wiliam, D. (2019) "Teaching not a research-based profession": https://www.tes.com/news/dylan-wiliam-teaching-not-research-based-profession

example research into practice. In Chapters 4 and 8, I will even share ways in which my own teaching at times deviates from this routine. Still, the routine in this chapter is the one I come back to most often.

From a combination of experience and research I know there are a lot of ways for a worked example activity to go wrong:

- Students might not understand the question.
- They might not pay attention to the solution.
- They might be overwhelmed by a poorly written solution.
- They might study the solution superficially and fail to truly understand it.
- They might understand the solution, but only see it as a solution for *this* problem. In other words, they leave with narrow and inflexible learning.

I have landed on a routine that tries to address as many of these concerns as possible. It's certainly not the only way to turn the concerns of research into a classroom activity, but it's the one I personally rely on the most.

Research points to specific activities that help students engage deeply with a worked-out solution: we can ask students to **analyze** the solution, prompt them to **explain** it in detail, and then give chances to **apply** the solution to a new problem (see Chapter 1). This routine is built on these principles, but fleshed-out based on my own values and context.

The routine goes like this:
1. I slowly reveal the solution.
2. I give quiet time for studying the solution.
3. I ask students to carefully explain the solution with a partner. I ask them to answer specific questions about it.
4. I ask students to use the ideas from the solution to solve a new problem.

The next chapter will discuss some of the questions I've often received about this routine. For this chapter I will stick to detailing the steps I use to introduce a new worked example, from start to finish.

SLOW REVEAL OF THE SOLUTION

"Welcome to class everyone," I'll say. "There's a problem waiting for you on the board. Take a look and try to solve it as soon as you can." This is the problem I've posted:

These polygons have been divided into triangles with diagonals coming out of one vertex:

How many triangles would be formed if you divided a 10-sided polygon in this way?

Bonus: What about a polygon with 100 sides? N sides?

This question is one the class has already studied, so it's a type of review. I'm starting class with it both because practice and review are important, but also because it is deeply connected to the example that I'm about to share. Today's lesson is about finding the sum of the interior angles of a polygon, and I want to use this "triangulation" technique to help find it.

Problems such as these can help students **notice** and **remember** information that will appear in the example (see Chapter 1). In this case, I'd like students to notice the details of the diagrams – the diagonals stemming from a single vertex, in particular. I'd also like them to remember the pattern that we studied in previous classes – that this "triangulation" produces 4 triangles for a 6-sided shape, 9 triangles for an 11-sided shape, n – 2 for an n-sided polygon. This will be so important for what's to come.

The class wraps up their work on this problem and I call on a student to share their solution. Then, I transition into the worked example. "Over the last few days we have been studying diagonals in polygons. Today we're going to use those same ideas to find the angle sum of *any* polygon. We're going to start by studying a solution to a tricky problem."

I use a document camera as often as I can in my classes, as it helps me quickly share and annotate images for my students. I'll shift the page with the example under the document camera but cover up as much of the solution as I can. "Under my hand is the solution to this problem. The problem is to find the angle sum of these shapes." Or if I have a blank copy of the problem handy, without a solution, I'll show it to my students first:

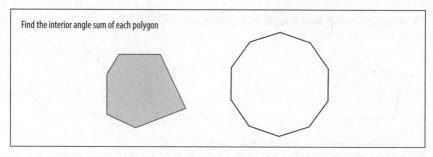

Find the interior angle sum of each polygon

Sometimes, I'll pause here for a moment so students can read the problem. It's very important that students understand what the question means before I reveal the solution. If I'm worried that students aren't really taking in the problem, I might pepper them with a few questions. "In your head, you might want to think whether you already have an approach to this problem." Other times I'll ask students to estimate: "What's your best guess as to the angle sum? Do you think it's more or less than 360 degrees?"

"More!" says one student. "Less," says another. "You're just guessing," I say. "Let's look at the solution."

No matter what though, I try to move briskly through this stage. It's crucial that students understand the question and what it's asking, but the real work is ahead.

TIME TO QUIETLY ANALYZE THE EXAMPLE

"I'm going to uncover the solution now, and I'd like you to read it all the way through." I will now ask students to **analyze** the example thoroughly.

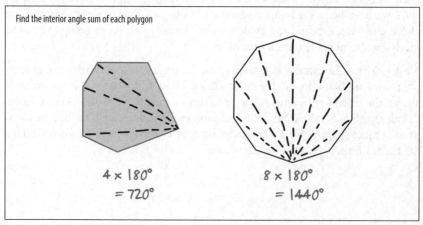

Find the interior angle sum of each polygon

$$4 \times 180°$$
$$= 720°$$

$$8 \times 180°$$
$$= 1440°$$

"Explain each step to yourself as best as you can. Put a thumb up when you've finished reading, even if there are parts of the solution you don't fully understand yet." (If you don't say this, some kids will just keep staring at the example. You won't know whether they are intently studying the example or spaced very far out.)

I try to write examples so that the information can be taken in without any speaking on my part. This is, of course, not always possible, but I find it a helpful design goal.

Research names many ways that examples can overload the cognitive resources students bring to the activity. Unnecessary words, redundant explanations, and necessary text that is separated from the diagram are among the most common, but they hardly exhaust the list (see Chapter 7). Learning something new is often an all-hands-on-deck situation, cognitively speaking, and I want to be careful. If the solutions I share require an explanation, I find the point can get lost in the explanation, and the entire activity drags on.

Instead, I aim to include as few steps as possible in the solution and try to get at the mathematical point very succinctly.

At this point, the room is silent. Students are not speaking, they are reading. But what is going on in their heads? Do they truly comprehend the example? It is impossible to be sure, though I've learned to pay attention to my students' eyes. When things are really working well, everybody is staring straight ahead at the example on the board. No one is looking down at their desk or across the room. Teachers are sometimes uncomfortable with silence in the classroom, and feel a reflexive need to speak when things get quiet. I try to resist that urge. There is deep silence in the room, but silence can help us think more clearly.

I have prompted students to explain each line of the solution for themselves, step by step. Research and experience agree that students sometimes study examples superficially. They often gloss over important details, telling themselves they understand it better than they actually do. (Honestly, this is something we're all guilty of.)

In Chapter 1, I shared research suggesting that self-explanation is the difference between students who are able and unable to learn from examples. Chi et al. asked students to speak aloud as they studied examples.[37] They then gave those students

---

37. Chi, M. T., Bassok, M., Lewis, M. W., Reimann, P., & Glaser, R. (1989) "Self-explanations: How students study and use examples in learning to solve problems," *Cognitive Science*, 13 (2), 145–182.

a test to see which had learned from the examples. They found that successful students read examples differently than their peers in the following ways:

1. **Self-awareness:** While reading an example, more successful students did a better job at realizing they *didn't* understand parts of what they were reading.

2. **Self-explanation:** When they became aware of gaps in their understanding, these successful students attempted to *explain* parts of the solution they did not understand.

3. **Time:** As a side-effect, successful students spent *more* time studying solutions, compared to students who were less successful in learning from the example. (I see this all the time in the classroom – the students who finish reading an example the quickest are often those I'm most worried about.)

If the problem is that students don't engage in self-explanation, the solution is to prompt them to do so. "You should read it line-by-line. Ask yourself, can I explain why they did this? Notice where you aren't able to explain what they did."

You may have noticed that I frequently ask students to show me their thumbs rather than raise their hands. This is a little thing, but it makes a difference: I don't want people waving their arms around while students are trying to look at the board. That can be distracting.[38]

Once nearly every student's thumb is raised, it's time for the next step.

EXPLAIN TO A PARTNER

Even though I prompted students to explain each line of the solution, this is not enough. Some students will engage shallowly with the example anyway. Shallow engagement is a vicious cycle – students don't notice that there are parts they don't understand, so they see no reason to dig deeper. To address that, now I will explicitly draw their attention to important details in the solution they might have passed over.

I ask students to take turns explaining the solution to a partner. I quickly walk around the room, clarifying who students should work with for the upcoming task. "Turn to your partner and take turns explaining each step of the solution until you both understand it all. Then, answer the questions together."

---

38. Parrish, S. (2014) *Number Talks: Whole Number Computation*. Math Solutions Publications.

1. Study this.	2. Answer these.
Find the interior angle sum of each polygon 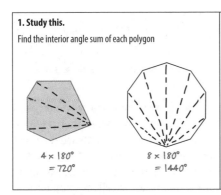 $4 \times 180°$ $= 720°$ $8 \times 180°$ $= 1440°$	• Why did they only draw the diagonals coming out of one vertex? • How come there are 6 sides on the left shape but only 4 triangles? • What if there were 7 sides? How would the diagram change?

My use of specific prompts is an idea borrowed from research – I first saw it in materials created by the Algebra by Example project, and it's supported by Chi et al.'s work (Chapter 1). The idea is to push students towards explaining ideas they might not even have realized they don't understand. It's also a useful chance to ask students to dig deeper and answer some "why" questions that can connect a procedure to concepts.

SOME GOOD PROMPTS

What makes for a good self-explanation prompt? "Avoid only asking 'what' questions," is the advice given by McGinn, Lange and Booth.[39] "Instead, focus on asking 'why' questions. You want to have students explain their reasoning, not just state the procedure."

Procedural and conceptual questions are both clearly important, but the procedural questions will likely be easier for students to answer. Push students to think harder by asking them to explain "why" and "what if" questions.

McGinn, Lange and Booth provide a list of sample prompts for teachers to adapt. Here are some of my favorites from their list:

"What did [student name] do as his first step?"

"Would it have been OK to write _____? Why or why not?"

"Why did [student name] combine _____ and

_____?"

---

39. McGinn, K. M., Lange, K. E., & Booth, J. L. (2015) "A worked example for creating worked examples," *Mathematics Teaching in the Middle School*, 21 (1), 26–33.

> "Would [student name] have gotten the same answer if they
> _____ first?"
>
> "Explain why _____ would have been an unreasonable answer."

As we've seen, research suggests that students may not know what good explanation (or self-explanation) looks like.[40] There are two ways that research has attempted to address this concern. The first is to teach students what a great response to these prompts would look like – how a good explanation connects particular details of a solution to rules or principles that are true across many problems. To do this we can analyze an example of an excellent explanation. There is a virtuous cycle at play here: to learn from examples, we need to self-explain; we can also learn how to self-explain well from examples.

The other suggestion of research is to create highly structured self-explanation prompts. Researchers have found positive effects using fill-in-the-blank prompts such as these:[41]

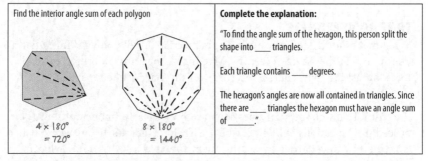

Find the interior angle sum of each polygon	Complete the explanation:
$4 \times 180°$ $= 720°$ $\quad$ $8 \times 180°$ $= 1440°$	"To find the angle sum of the hexagon, this person split the shape into ____ triangles. Each triangle contains ____ degrees. The hexagon's angles are now all contained in triangles. Since there are ____ triangles the hexagon must have an angle sum of _____."

These same researchers have also found benefits from asking students to choose between a menu of explanations, one of which fits the example well. When doing this, the choice should be between two legitimate mathematical principles – the point is for students to focus on turning a particular example into a generally useful rule. For the lesson my students are studying, a menu prompt might look like this:

40. Rittle-Johnson, B., Loehr, A. M., & Durkin, K. (2017) "Promoting self-explanation to improve mathematics learning: A meta-analysis and instructional design principles," *ZDM*, 49 (4), 599–611.
41. Berthold, K., Eysink, T. H., & Renkl, A. (2009) "Assisting self-explanation prompts are more effective than open prompts when learning with multiple representations," *Instructional Science*, 37 (4), 345–363.

Find the interior angle sum of each polygon	Which best explains the example?
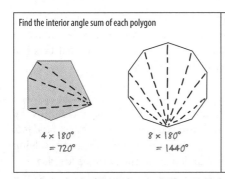 $4 \times 180°$ $= 720°$ $\qquad$ $8 \times 180°$ $= 1440°$	a. When a polygon is split into triangles by diagonals coming out of one vertex, there are always two fewer triangles than sides. Since each triangle contains 180 degrees, the angle sum is 180 times the number of sides minus 2. b. The interior angle sum of a quadrilateral is always 360 degrees, so we can simply continue adding 180 degrees to it to find angle sums for larger polygons.

Whether the prompt comes in the form of a question, a "fill-in-the-blank" or a menu, I almost always ask my students to talk to each other about the solution and these prompts using "turn and talk." I assign partners and ask students to discuss the task in pairs, before returning to address the class all at once. There are a number of reasons I do this:

- To give students a chance to ask either me or their partner a question.
- So that I can listen in on partners' discussions and get a feel for whether students are understanding the solution.
- When students reach a step that they can't explain, they realize they need to study the example more closely.
- When students are able to explain the solution fully, their thinking becomes more organized and they are more ready to apply it in the future.
- To give me a sense of whether I would like to lead a discussion about any aspect of this, or whether students seem ready to move on to the next stage.
- To help give me an idea of which students I would like to call on to share ideas during the follow-up discussion.

That last point is an important one for me. I love hearing students share their mathematical thinking, but I grow deeply concerned about who gets to speak during discussions. Isn't it usually the most confident students who benefit from these discussions? It's important to get even the least confident students speaking in class, so they know their mathematical thinking is valuable and interesting. The issue with calling on students with a lack of confidence, however, is that they aren't confident! They are caught in a cycle of silence, afraid to share thinking in public because they rarely get the chance to.

This routine helps me break the cycle. I can give students a chance to practice explaining ideas with their partners before asking them to take center stage. I can even let them know that I intend to call on them. I can make sure they know that their ideas are correct and valuable, and then I can give them a chance to prove it in front of the whole class. I want every student to know that this is a classroom where, mathematically speaking, they belong.

YOUR TURN

While students were speaking, I was handing out pages. The page contains the example, the explanation prompts, and some unsolved problems. I now ask students to **apply** what they have learned to a new case. "As soon as you're ready, try solving these problems on your own. If you're stuck, look back to the example for ideas."

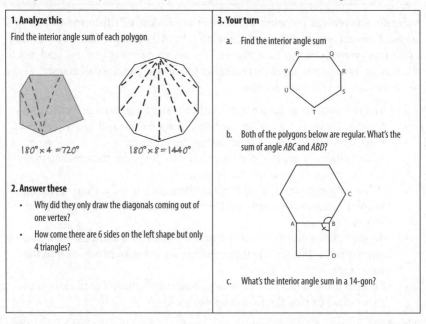

This is straight out of the research playbook. John Sweller called this instructional format "example-problem pairs," and used it in many of his experiments.[42] By pairing solved problems with unsolved ones, I get a very quick sense of whether students understood the example. Students do as well. While it is possible to fool yourself into thinking you understand each part of a solution, it's much harder to tell yourself you can solve a problem when you can't! Trouble with the problem sometimes prompts students to go back and study the example more carefully.

42. Sweller, J., Ayres, P., & Kalyuga, S. (2011) *Cognitive Load Theory*. Springer New York.

John Sweller originally paired examples with problems to help motivate students to pay careful attention to the examples.[43] That's one reason why a "Your Turn" section is important, but there are many other reasons as well:

- It allows me to assess whether students have gotten the point and are ready for more.
- Solving problems is an engaging, energizing way to give students a chance to feel as if the idea they have read about is truly their own.
- I never make the problems exactly like those shown in the example. Because students know they are going to use the idea from the example in the solution, I can vary the problem just a bit. (But not too much!) This helps students make generalizations that will help them apply this to many more problems in the future.

HOW DIFFERENT SHOULD THE PROBLEM BE FROM THE SOLUTION?

Researchers have studied the benefits of making the "Your Turn" problem more or less similar to the studied example.[44] There appears to be a bit of a Goldilocks problem – we need just the right amount of variation to get the full benefits.

Make the problem too different from the example and students will be unable to solve the problem. Make it too similar, and students will fail to form a solid generalization, and end up seeing the solution as applying only to a narrow case.

There is no single formula for creating the right amount of variation between the example and the solution. Often, though, I find it helpful to change *just one thing* between the example and the problem. It can be the order an equation is written in, the number of sides in the polygon, or the exponent a number is raised to. When I try to change more than one thing at once, I often find my students struggle to apply what they have just learned to the problem.

---

43. Sweller, J., & Cooper, G. A. (1985) "The use of worked examples as a substitute for problem solving in learning algebra," *Cognition and Instruction*, 2 (1), 59–89.
44. Atkinson, R. K., Derry, S. J., Renkl, A., & Wortham, D (2000) "Learning from examples: Instructional principles from the worked examples research," *Review of Educational Research*, 70 (2), 181–214.

As students complete problems, I post answers on the board. I lag behind students just a bit, so that most have had a chance to try the problem before an answer appears. Students are growing familiar with something new – they'll want to know if they are on the right track, and rightly so. This bit of feedback can help students decide if they need to ask a question, and can help me decide who to approach to offer guidance.

Sometimes, there is controversy over the answer to one of these problems. In that case, we'll have a discussion. Otherwise, this is the end of the activity.

WHAT COMES NEXT?

This whole activity can take anywhere from five to twenty minutes, depending on the complexity of the topic, whether I lead the class in a discussion, and how many problems I have asked students to solve.

If the example was not too complex, we might study a second example during class. Rarely do I ask students to study more than two examples in a single class period, and whenever I do, I end up regretting it. There is only so much new material a student can take in without feeling overwhelmed.

There is probably no way to easily summarize the sorts of activities that we do after analyzing an example. Two points are important to mention, though:

- I try to continue to use the ideas from the example in the rest of the lesson. That way, students have a chance to continue using the idea in different contexts, strengthening their learning.
- I frequently follow the example activity with an activity that students would have found difficult if not for the example. For instance, a mixed-review practice set where students need to decide which strategy to use. Or a challenging application problem that students now have a strategy for, after having studied the example.

I don't use this routine every day. How frequently I use it depends on where we are in the unit. When we are at the start of a new topic, though, I do use it daily.

IN SHORT

- Teaching will never be fully determined by evidence – it's too complex. But **evidence can inform teaching** in rich ways.
- To help students **notice** and **remember** information needed for analyzing the example, I often **start with a review problem** that today's example will build on.
- To help students **analyze** a solution, **I reveal an example slowly and create quiet conditions** so students can give it their full attention.
- To encourage students to **explain** the example, I ask them to **think about and discuss explanation prompts.** Many of my prompts focus on the "why" more than the "how."
- I ask students to **apply** the solution by **solving new problems** that are different – but not too different – from the problem in the worked example.

CHAPTER 4: SOME QUESTIONS AND ANSWERS ABOUT THE ROUTINE

Here are some of the questions that people frequently have about the routine from Chapter 3, along with my answers.

Q: When do students take notes?

A: I don't ask students to take notes on the examples. In my classes, the example handout is the notes, and I don't believe there are learning benefits of asking students to copy it down in their own notebooks.

We have had lively discussions about this in my department at school. I know this is somewhat controversial! But hear me out.

On the one hand, there is research supporting the idea that taking notes can help learning. But it's not magic; the benefits only come when notes cause students to think about the material. Carolina Kuepper-Tetzel, an experimental psychologist, summarizes the research on note-taking in the following way:

> Generally, the functions of note-taking are two-fold: First, taking notes can have a positive effect on the intake and processing of information (*encoding effect*). The idea of this is that while we take notes, we engage actively with the content of a lecture or class, which leads to better comprehension of the presented material. The second function is that notes allow learners to go back to them and use them to study the material (*external storage effect*).[45]

Taking notes benefits us when it helps us engage more actively with the content than we otherwise would, either now or later. The question is whether, in the course of my routine, taking notes would help.

As far as "later" is concerned, I provide students with a solution on a handout. True, they don't have a notebook containing every definition and procedure we cover in class. But they *do* have a binder containing all of our handouts, including these handouts with worked examples. That binder is required – I provide it at the start of the year. Students can restudy from a handout just as well as from notes.

---

45. Kuepper-Tetzel, C. "Factors of effective note-taking: Application of cognitive load theory": https://www.learningscientists.org/blog/2018/9/13-1

53

When it comes to the "now," we have to consider the costs of taking notes, and not just the potential benefits. Copying notes down, after all, takes time. While students are copying the board into their notebooks, it seems to me they are not thinking much about the mathematics. They are splitting their attention across two different writing surfaces, something that especially taxes one's mental resources.[46] They aren't given time to self-explain, and there is no requirement to consolidate or summarize the material. (Summarizing or organizing is the kind of active engagement with content that studies about notes support.) Copying a solution off the board is not very useful for learning.

From my point of view, I am replacing copying with superior learning activities. Rather than take time on copying the board, I ask students to engage more actively with a solution by studying it, explaining how it works in detail, and then applying it on their own. Obviously any individual act of note-taking doesn't take very long, but it all adds up.

With all that said, this is not a hill on which I am prepared to die. Many of my colleagues ask their students to take notes, and that's fine by me. My school is also very generous in allowing me to photocopy as much as I need for class. I have taught at other places that imposed limits on how much a teacher is allowed to copy, making notes strictly necessary.

Q: Do students write down the answers to the self-explanation prompts, or only discuss them with classmates?
A: I usually ask students to answer the questions in writing on the handout with the example on it. For some students, the writing helps them gather their thoughts more clearly.

Q: Do you always start the routine with a review problem for students to solve?
A: No, only if there is information I want students to notice or remember before they study the example.

Q: It seems you don't explain the example to the students before they have studied it. Why is that?
A: I don't always explain each step of the example to the class. In fact, initially I prefer not to. But sometimes it is necessary – especially when the material is very complex – and then I happily explain the process of solving the problem for students.

I like my students to try to make sense of a solution on their own. Too often when a teacher voices an explanation it is easy to pretend you understand

---

46. Mayer, R. E. (2002) "Multimedia learning," *Psychology of Learning and Motivation*, 41, 85–139.

things that you don't. I want to give students a chance to notice the gaps in their understanding, and to address them by studying the example more carefully. Plus, my students find it enjoyable to understand new solutions. I like giving them the chance to explain the solution on their own.

None of this would work if the solution wasn't fully worked-out. I work hard to create solutions that students can learn from all on their own. In this, I am imitating the conditions that researchers have created while studying worked examples – they almost always present a solution with no explanation at all.

There is another reason I don't explain right away: I want students to have a chance to read mathematics in class. Reading mathematics is different than reading a novel or the newspaper. It takes careful, line-by-line engagement with the text. It's important not to skim over the tough parts; those are the parts that are probably the most crucial. To read mathematics well is to provide your own commentary as you go. I hope that my class is a place where a student can get used to this kind of technical reading.

I've never felt good about leaving students hanging, though. If someone doesn't understand a solution, I will certainly explain each step. I just aim to create solutions that my students can understand on their own, without my explanation.

An important addendum to all of this will come in Chapter 8, where I'll discuss teaching proof with worked-out examples. When I teach complex topics, such as geometrical proof, I find it is often impossible to capture the entire mathematical idea in the worked example itself. When teaching these topics it is important to explain the process of creating the end-result for students – otherwise, the work I'm presenting will seem like a mystery to my class. I won't wait for students to explain the work on their own in these situations.

Q: In your routine, you first ask students to study a solution. Then, when everyone is finished, you reveal prompts for explanation. Wouldn't revealing them with the solution help students read it more carefully?

A: It's already a lot of work to make sense of the solution up on the board. And when students start thinking about those explanation prompts, inevitably some will ask to write them down. I prefer to keep everyone's focus on the board – it's much easier to encourage students to study a solution when everyone is doing so, and nobody is fiddling with pencils or paper.

Sometimes I'll reveal those self-explanation prompts early, if I get the sense that some students are ready to move on but others need more time. But usually I keep those prompts hidden at first.

Q: Do you leave the example up when students try to solve the "Your Turn" application problem?

A: Yes, absolutely. I always make sure the example is visible to students when I ask them to apply it. Even though we have just analyzed an example closely, students often will need a visual reminder of what they have just studied. That's normal – the mathematics is brand new. Moreover, students can learn a lot from trying to adapt a solution from an example to a new problem. The more time that students spend closely analyzing the example, the better. Looking at a correct example and trying to adapt it to a new problem is an entirely sensible way for beginners to learn how to solve it.

Students will have plenty of time to practice solving problems without an example present later in our lesson and unit – at this early stage, I want students to have a solution to study from if they need it.

Q: Does your routine work for online learning?

A: It does, with modifications.

Like much of the teaching world, I turned to online teaching during the coronavirus pandemic in March 2020. I found I was mostly able to preserve my worked example routine, thanks to the chat box.

I would slowly reveal the solution, at first only showing the question. Then I would reveal the solution and ask students to either raise a thumb or type into the chat when they had finished reading it. I would then post self-explanation prompts. Students can't easily explain ideas to each other during a video conference. Instead, I set the chat functionality so that students could only chat with me. I asked students to send me their answers to the explanation prompts. I would thank students as their messages came in, and sometimes I would post a particularly clear explanation on the screen for other students to see. Then I would assign a problem for students to try on their own and again ask them to send me their responses.

Across the globe, very little went smoothly during the pandemic. I was relieved that this little bit of my teaching life continued to operate more or less as intended.

Q: Does it matter whether you associate the solution with a particular fictional student (e.g. "This is how Michael solved the problem")?

A: The Algebra by Example project that I so admire always presents a solution as the work of a fictional student. But there is research to suggest that there are risks to presenting examples in this way.

In a research study with a truly excellent title ("Does it matter how Molly does it?"), Riggs et al. gave one group of middle-school students a solution that was linked to a person.[47] The other group received the same solution, but without any name attached. The students who studied the solution without any name attached were *more* likely to use the new strategy when presented with a similar problem.

Riggs et al. offered two possible explanations for this result. The first is that the additional name distracted students somewhat from the solution. This seems to be more of a concern if you really build up a profile of the person: "Rose is a construction worker who needs to use angles *all the time*. She sometimes needs to measure them, etc." And textbooks really do this sometimes, though they probably should not.

The second possibility – the one the researchers seem to prefer – is that linking a name to a strategy changes how we think about it. Add Molly's name to a strategy, and suddenly we don't think of it as *our* strategy that we have to learn. We think of it as *Molly's* approach; maybe it's not universally applicable or useful. Perhaps we simply do things differently than Molly does. A little part of us, the researchers suggest, doesn't think we'll ever need to use it after we study it. We don't think about it as broadly useful.

I have noticed this phenomenon at times. You invest a real chunk of class time towards studying a solution and then the next day... no one seems to remember to use it.

Mostly I have experienced this in two situations. The first is when students already have one way to solve the problem, and I am trying to teach them a more efficient method. (This was the situation in the study.) When students have no other way to solve a problem, I think they're less likely to fall into the "Molly's solution" trap. I've also found this occurs most often when the solution comes from an *actual* Molly in my class, not a fictional one. The more real the person is, the easier it is to think of a solution as belonging just to them, I think.

Truth be told, I do often use fictional names for strategies in class. I suspect that when you use examples over and over in class, your students get the picture. They learn that when you present a solution that it really matters, and they are expected to learn to use it in the future. This may be a difference between the research and my context, since the researchers dropped in on classrooms just once.

---

47. Riggs, A. E., Alibali, M. W., & Kalish, C. W. (2017) "Does it matter how Molly does it? Person-presentation of strategies and transfer in mathematics," *Contemporary Educational Psychology*, 51, 315–320.

Why use names at all? They aren't so important to me, but I do find them convenient for the sake of discussion. "Who can explain why Hana added 7 to both sides?" is easy to ask. Without a name, I sometimes trip over the language: "Who can explain why in the example there is a 7 added to both sides?" This is wordy and uses the passive. I'd rather avoid it.

A possible compromise is to use meaningful labels rather than names. Rather than "Here's what Molly did," we might say "Here's the balancing method." It's a bit more of a mouthful during discussions, but it clarifies for students that this strategy belongs to them, rather than someone else.

I don't know if I'm going to change my teaching because of Riggs et al.'s paper, but I love it. It is provocative for me, in the best sense of that word. It has made me aware of something I otherwise never would have thought about, and will probably impact my teaching in subtle ways for years to come.

Q: Is your routine the only good way to present worked examples?
A: No, it is *not* the only good way.

There are certainly other routines for learning from examples in class. Not long ago, I found myself needing to improvise a worked example in class. I thought for a moment, and then wrote a problem on the board. "This is the sort of problem we've been studying in class. I'm going to write a solution on the board. I'm not going to say a word while I do this – it's going to be absolutely silent."

I wrote the solution on the board, and then I stepped away without saying a word. "Turn to your partner and explain each line of this solution." Everything else proceeded according to my usual routine.

I didn't come up with this "silent teacher" idea; I learned of it from Craig Barton, who describes it in his book *How I Wish I'd Taught Maths*.[48] (Apparently, "The Silent Teacher" was a bit of a teaching fad in the UK around 2012. Lord knows we have fads in the US, though this one didn't seem to make it to where I taught.) He delivers the examples in silence to reduce distractions and redundant information.

Those are the same concerns that drove me to produce a slightly different routine for my own teaching. No matter. There is more than one way to skin a cat, and I sometimes use Craig's routine, especially when I find myself improvising examples in class.

---

48. Barton, C. (2018) *How I Wish I'd Taught Maths: lessons learned from research, conversations with experts, and 12 years of mistakes.* John Catt Educational.

As I mentioned above, the routine also depends on the content. As material becomes more difficult to represent in writing, it becomes crucial for the teacher to add in explanatory details. Beyond these factors, every teacher's school context and personality is different, and we should never expect total convergence in practices. Different routines can be created that address similar concerns, informed by the same evidence, and are similarly grounded in classroom experience. There are surely other good routines for presenting solutions in class, waiting to be discovered by thoughtful classroom teachers.

IN SHORT

- **Notes are only effective if they promote active thinking in students,** either before or after the lesson. Because I provide handouts and push students to think during the lesson itself, **I don't ask students to also take notes.**
- **By waiting to explain, the teacher allows students to engage deeply with the solution on their own.** But the teacher must ensure that every student understands the solution, and should explain the solution if need be. Waiting to explain only works when the full mathematical idea can be presented to students in the example – **when an idea can't be easily shared in writing, teachers should explain it to students.**
- The routine is adaptable to online contexts.
- There is solid research that suggests when strategies are associated with particular people ("Molly's solution") students do not apply them to new contexts as often. I find it useful to **associate strategies with fictional names** anyway, but it's important to be aware of the risks.
- There are many ways to bring research on worked examples into practice. My own routine is not the only great way to teach with worked examples.

CHAPTER 5: MOVING FROM EXAMPLES TO PROBLEM SOLVING

George Pólya, mathematician and author, wrote in his preface to *Mathematical Discovery* that "solving problems is a practical art, like swimming or skiing, or playing the piano: you can learn it only by imitation and practice."[49] We imitate our teachers at first, and then gain independence by practicing what we have learned from teachers on our own.

We might agree with Pólya in principle while still thinking, practically speaking, that a lot of activities combine elements of imitation and practice. Some of the best teaching I have seen exists in the middle zone between full guidance and complete independence. Especially as skills become more complex, independent practice becomes challenging to even attempt. Imagine a swim class whose instructor takes a lap in the water while the students watch. The instructor returns and they discuss what he did. He asks, "Any questions?" and encourages his students to dive in. That's a recipe for a lot of sinking students.

I've already described in previous chapters how I use example-problem pairs in class. But for complex content there are two difficulties I've experienced with example-problem pairs:

- Students don't even understand what the question is asking, so they can't appreciate its solution.
- Students aren't able to move into practice problems after studying an example, because the skill contains many challenging sub-skills that are not yet automatic.

In this chapter I'll share some practice activities that address these two issues. These activities are all different, but share an important quality. They create practice settings where students see the entire solution and focus on improving at just part of it at once. To better understand the advantages of this approach, I find it useful to consider a distinction derived from research: the difference between whole-task and part-task practice. We'll discuss the distinction first, then move to the particular classroom strategies.

---

49. Pólya, G. (1981) *Mathematical Discovery: On understanding, learning, and teaching problem solving.* Wiley.

WHOLE-TASK AND PART-TASK PRACTICE

Van Merriënboer et al. describe two different types of practice tasks: whole-task practice and part-task practice.[50] In **part-task practice**, we practice the component parts of a complex skill. If a skill requires performing A then B then C in sequence, a part-task approach would involve practicing A, B and C each on their own. When I took piano lessons, my teacher often had me practice just a few tricky notes in just one hand. Once I could perform them flawlessly, we'd move on to the next difficult section. That's part-task practice.

Whole-task practice involves doing a simplified version of the whole thing you're trying to learn. Riding a stationary bike is part-task practice, but riding a bicycle with training wheels is whole-task practice. So is practicing a piano piece at an extremely slow tempo. Van Merriënboer and Kester describe these as "very simple but meaningful wholes."[51] They are meaningful because students can see how this activity relates to the thing they're ultimately trying to learn.

It's clearly not an either/or choice between part- and whole-task practice. You need both, especially as skills get more complex. Returning to the piano, practicing just a few notes in your right hand can help you play them nearly automatically. That's fantastic. But to play the piece correctly, you'll have to play that in the right hand *while* also playing something in the left. That's not a simple thing for a young piano student. A good piano teacher will help students practice this shift from one-handed to two-handed play.

The distinction between part- and whole-task, I have to admit, gets fuzzy at times. Many activities can be thought of as meaningful wholes while *also* being just part of more complex ones. It's also worth noting that researchers usually discuss this distinction when talking about physical or professional training – things like riding a bike or diagnosing a patient where you're called on to perform many different skills at once. Research doesn't usually apply this framework to the learning of mathematical skills, many of which require less simultaneous coordination.

Still, I find the distinction a useful lens to apply to my own work. It's true that a lot of mathematical procedures can be split up into several discrete steps. On the face of things, this suggests you could study them entirely through their parts. But that would cause trouble for students. Even if a skill looks like "A then B then C," very often you need to be thinking about B while you're doing A. Very

---

50. Van Merriënboer, J. J., Kirschner, P. A., & Kester, L. (2003) "Taking the load off a learner's mind: Instructional design for complex learning," *Educational Psychologist*, 38 (1), 5–13.

51. Van Merriënboer, J. J., & Kester, L. (2008) "Whole-task models in education," *Handbook of Research on Educational Communications and Technology*, 3, 441–456.

often, strategic decisions about *how* to perform A depend on what your needs will be when performing B. Moreover, it is difficult to learn meaningless steps, and often a step in a procedure is pointless unless you know where it's headed.

It makes sense that, besides practicing A on its own, you'd also want to practice doing A in a context where you can also think about B. That's whole-task practice.

One of the trickiest skills I teach my eighth graders is solving systems of equations. In the easiest case, the solution still involves at least three distinctive sub-goals. Consider this system of equations:

$$y = 9x + 4$$

$$y = 11x$$

To solve this system via substitution, you have to perform three steps:

1. Set the equations equal.
2. Solve the resulting equation.
3. Plug in the solution to find the other number.

A typical class will have already practiced steps 2 and 3 on their own before trying to solve a system. The last part left to practice is the first, setting equations equal to each other. But students could be forgiven for finding it a bit mysterious why you'd do that first step, unless they could see where the rest of the solution is headed. It's hard to remember three disconnected steps. It's easier if you can practice them in context.

As the unit proceeds, students learn that there are two ways to solve a system of linear equations: substitution and elimination. Each strategy is more or less useful for different systems. To learn to choose wisely, students need to think about the upcoming steps. They need to work on this part of the skill in its natural context.

I've always felt fairly confident in my ability to put together part-task practice for students. What has taken me longer is finding practice formats that *meaningfully preserve the whole, while letting students practice just a part*. That's the sort of practice that I find is often missing from otherwise solid teaching. When needed, it can help bridge the gap between examples and problem solving.

Note that this is one of the advantages of starting with worked examples. You get the full context, right from the start. Studying a worked example is whole-task practice. The question is how we can move from worked examples to independent problem solving while still employing whole-task practice.

There are five types of learning activity that I find most useful for this purpose. They complement worked examples, and many of them even blur the line between solutions and problems. They are:

- Meaning-making problems
- Completion problems
- Fading out an example
- Comparing two strategies
- Mistake analysis

TECHNIQUE 1: MEANING-MAKING PROBLEMS

Even though worked examples work best earlier in a unit, it's often a bad idea to study a solution as the first activity on day 1. The issue arises when students don't know enough to understand the worked example.

After several years of frustration, I realized just how hard it is for students to understand what a system of equations is. All their experiences up until this point have usually been in solving one-variable equations. How can you learn to find the solution to something if you don't even understand what it is?

I know that my students are familiar with Venn Diagrams. Under the hood, Venn Diagrams and systems of equations operate using a similar logic. There are two conditions, and we are interested in something that satisfies both conditions at once. Venn Diagrams can be a useful way to think about what it means to solve a system.

To start a unit that involves systems of equations – before asking my students to study any solutions – I'll share this image:

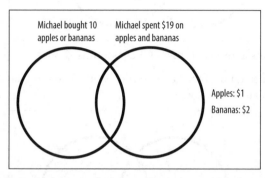

"What are some combinations of apples or bananas I might have bought?" I ask. "Raise your hand if you have an idea."

"5 and 5!" one student says.

"6 apples and 4 bananas," says another.

"10 apples and 0 bananas," says a third.

"We're getting the hang of the left side," I say. "What about on the right? The second clue – the second constraint – is that I spent $19 on all the fruit I purchased. So, what might I have bought? I'll go first: 5 apples and 7 bananas." I write (5, 7) inside the right circle.

I take more suggestions from students and record them in the second circle. Then, I put question marks in the overlapping region of the diagram. "We've found a bunch of numbers that satisfy the first clue, and a bunch more that have satisfied the second. Is there anything that satisfies both clues at once?"

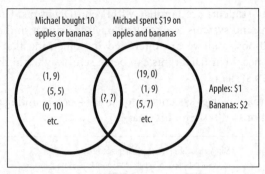

Quickly, students agree: (1, 9) fits both constraints at once.

After they understand how these puzzles work, I ask my students to solve several of them all on their own.

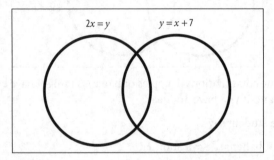

I like these Venn problems because they provide a clear answer to the question, "what does it mean to solve a system?" It's true that students can only approach this problem with inefficient, sometimes frustrating methods. My goal with these problems is not for students to learn how to solve a system, though. I simply want to give them a meaningful, whole-task opportunity to learn what a system *is*. I call these "meaning-making problems" because their aim is to teach what the problem means and what it means to solve it, but not how to solve it.

Researchers who favor worked examples have suggested that problem solving can be useful when used in this way. Kalyuga and Singh note that most studies find benefits when people study worked examples to learn new content, rather than spend time solving problems.[52] But some researchers consistently find benefits for students who attempt problems before studying a solution. Kalyuga and Singh attempt to square these divergent results by suggesting it depends

52. Kalyuga, S., & Singh, A. M. (2016) "Rethinking the boundaries of cognitive load theory in complex learning," *Educational Psychology Review*, 28 (4), 831–852.

on your goal. If you want to help students understand what a problem is asking and what it would mean to solve it, then trying a problem can be a good way to gain that knowledge.

Research doesn't suggest benefits increase through spending a ton of time on this, and that matches my experience. Students don't have efficient ways to solve the problem – a good thing for them to notice! – and they can quickly grow frustrated with the search for solutions. (Though if a group is having fun with the problems, I don't mind letting them struggle at it for a bit longer.) My aim isn't to teach them how to solve the problem at this stage. I have worked examples for that, and it's what I turn the class to next.

TECHNIQUE 2: COMPLETION PROBLEMS

What happens after a worked example if students aren't able to jump into solving the full problem on their own? I find completion problems a fantastic next step for just this situation.

A "completion problem" is a worked example with missing steps. Students are asked to fill in the blanks. It's focused practice within a meaningful setting. Here is one that I use with my students during the systems of equations unit:

Complete the solution:

$$y = 2x + 3 \text{ and } y = 5x - 6$$
$$2x + 4 = 5x - 8$$
$$4 = 3x - 8$$
$$12 = 3x$$
$$x = \underline{\quad\quad}$$
$$y = \underline{\quad\quad}$$

I cited the Dutch researcher Jeroen van Merriënboer at the start of this chapter. In 1990, Van Merriënboer wrote a paper that introduced completion problems to the world of worked examples research. He ran a study involving high-school students who were learning to write computer programs. When given a sample computer program and an assignment to try on their own, many students were eager to try the assignment. As a result, the students in Van Merriënboer's experiments tended to "skip over the examples, not study them at all, or only start searching for examples that fit in with their solution when they experience[d] serious difficulties in solving a programming problem." His solution was to delete lines of code in the sample program for students to complete on their own – that's a completion problem. Students who completed the sample program outperformed the other group of students, who were tasked with studying worked-out computer programs.[53]

I love that completion problems exist somewhere between imitation and practice. The format makes students sweat the small stuff, but that work is embedded in a meaningful context. These two ideas of Van Merriënboer's – whole-task practice and completion problems – are deeply connected.

Here are some things I keep in mind while putting together a completion problem:

- I like to make the completion problem a bit more difficult than the most recent worked example. Otherwise, the worked-out portion of the problem can feel a bit samey, and I like to keep things moving along.
- If one step of a solution is particularly difficult for students to do on their own, at first I don't ask students to complete it. Instead, I'll ask students to complete a relatively easy step, knowing that this will also give them a chance to study the rest of the solution.
- Van Merriënboer reports students skimming over examples, but I don't really experience that in class. The reason is because of everything I do to motivate and engage students during my worked example routine (Chapters 3–5). Completion problems might be especially valuable in situations where there is no teacher present – they make excellent homework assignments.

One playful way to use completion problems, by the way, is to delete far too much of the solution and even some of the question, leaving students to create the problem while matching it up with the solution:

What could the problem have been?

$y = $ _____ and $y = $ _____

$6x = 2$

$x = 3$

$y = 4$

---

53. Van Merriënboer, J. J. (1990) "Strategies for programming instruction in high school: Program completion vs. program generation," *Journal of Educational Computing Research*, 6 (3), 265–285.

These sorts of problems are more open-ended than the "classic" completion problems. Since they ask students to think of a familiar problem in a different way, they can be useful as classroom challenges or as informal ways of checking what students understand.

TECHNIQUE 3: FADING OUT AN EXAMPLE

Completion problems are good, but they only focus on one step at a time. You'll need more than one of them to study each step of a skill. This might give you an idea: what if you could string together several completion problems, so that the sequence covers the entire skill?

Congratulations! You just invented "fading out an example."

Renkl et al. devised a systematic way to help students move from worked examples to solving problems.[54] They assigned a worked example. Then, they removed the last step of a similar example and asked students to complete it. Next, they deleted the final two steps of an example, and asked students to complete those. They proceeded this way until the entire example was deleted, save for the problem itself, which students would solve. The worked example slowly faded away, leaving a problem behind. Renkl et al. compared students who learned via the faded examples with students who used example-problem pairs. The students who studied faded-out examples outperformed the others.

I knew of this research, but for years I didn't try it in class. It seemed unnecessary to me, and maybe even overly didactic. That changed when I tried it out with a class struggling with systems of equations. Out of any better ideas, I remembered this research suggestion and figured it was worth a shot. This was the assignment I brought into class:

Complete the steps, solve the system

1.	2.	3.	4.
$-6x + y = -50$	$-10y = x$	$3x + 4y = 50$	$y = 2x$
$y = -4x$	$-5x - 7y = 43$	$-2x = y$	$-3x + 8y = 26$
$-6x + (-4x) = -50$	$-5(-10y) - 7y = 43$	$3x + 4(-2x) = 50$	
$-6x - 4x = -50$	$50y - 7y = 43$		
$-10x = -50$			
$x = 5$			
$y = \_\_\_$			

54. Renkl, A., Atkinson, R. K., Maier, U. H., & Staley, R. (2002) "From example study to problem solving: Smooth transitions help learning," *The Journal of Experimental Education*, 70 (4), 293–315.

As my class got to work, I was surprised by how challenging the assignment was. Students were asking me good questions about mechanical issues I hadn't even considered to be problematic for them. It turns out that lurking beneath their overall struggles had been a variety of smaller difficulties. The faded-out exercise gave them a chance to systematically work on *all of them*.

Many of my students made mistakes in the early steps. My student Lucy, for instance, had trouble from the start finding the second coordinate. But after getting help with that, she found the second coordinate like a pro on every subsequent problem.

Complete the steps, solve the system

1. $-6x + y = -50$	2. $-10y = x$	3. $3x + 4y = 50$	4. $y = 2x$
$y = -4x$	$-5x - 7y = 43$	$-2x = y$	$-3x + 8y = 26$
$-6x + (-4x) = -50$	$-5(-10y) - 7y = 43$	$3x + 4(-2x) = 50$	$-3x + 8(2x) = 26$
$-6x - 4x = -50$	$50y - 7y = 43$	$3x + -8x = 50$	$-3x + 16x = 26$
$-10x = -50$	$43y = 43$	$-5x = 50$	$13x = 26$
$x = 5$	$y = 1$	$x = -10$	$x = 2$
$y = -20$	$x = 10$	$y = 20$	$y = 4$

Each faded-out step gave Lucy a new step to focus on. She asked questions at each stage, looking back at previous examples when she wasn't sure where to go next. She solved the last problem entirely on her own. As the example faded away, her confidence grew.

I was worried that faded-out examples wouldn't be challenging enough. It turned out to be not just extremely challenging, but highly productive.

TECHNIQUE 4: CASE COMPARISONS

My students need to grow comfortable with two different ways of solving systems, commonly called solving by "substitution" and "elimination" in the US. One of the trickiest things to learn is *when* each approach is most appropriate. This is something I aim to explicitly coach my students in, once they have studied both approaches.

To do this, I ask students to compare different solutions to the same problem. "Here is how two students approached the same system of equations," I say to the class. "Study each of these, and put a thumb up when you've read them both."

Dana's solution	Jose's solution
$2x - y = 5$	$4x - 2y = 10$
$x + 2y = 15$	$x2 \quad 2x - y = 5 \quad x2$
$-2y \quad -2y$	$x + 2y = 15$
$x = 15 - 2y$	
$2(15 - 2y) - y = 5$	$5x \quad = 25$
$30 - 5y = 5$	$x = 5 \quad y = 5$
$-5y = -25$	
$y = 5, \ x = 5$	

Researchers sometimes call this a "case comparison." Alifieri et al. performed a systematic review of this literature and concluded that studies of case comparisons typically find benefits for students when compared to other ways of studying cases.[55] (This review wasn't primarily about math, fair warning.) They also went a step further and attempted to summarize factors that made these activities more effective in the studies they reviewed. Two of those suggestions I find helpful to remember:

- It's valuable to ask students to search for similarities between things that appear different. That's because there are many obvious differences on the surface, but it takes a bit of thought to see what they share.
- After studying the two approaches, students need help getting a "moral of the story" principle. It needs to be a generalization they can apply to other problems.

Based on this research, I asked my students to think about two questions after they read the case comparison given above:

1. What are some similarities between Dana and Jose's approaches?
2. Jose used the "elimination" strategy. Why might you prefer his approach?

Here are some of the similarities students may pick up on:

- Same answer.
- Similar final equations ($5x = 25$, $-5y = -25$).
- Both involve solving an equation.
- Both require substitution to find the value of the second variable.

---

55. Alfieri, L., Nokes-Malach, T. J., & Schunn, C. D. (2013) "Learning through case comparisons: A meta-analytic review," *Educational Psychologist*, 48 (2), 87–113.

Now that we've looked deeply for similarities, it's time to talk about differences. Here are reasons why Jose's approach may be preferable:

- It's shorter.
- It doesn't involve solving for a variable.
- You get a simple equation after just one step.
- You can match up the $+2y$ with $-2y$ just by multiplying the top equation by 2.

After these questions, I sum up: "When neither equation is solved for a variable, that's often a sign that elimination will be the simpler approach." (This is not a hard-and-fast rule. A student is not *wrong* if they choose an approach that many others find more difficult.)

Case comparisons are very effective at helping us focus on subtle decisions that are often untaught. It is another whole-task practice format. The part-task practice version of a case comparison might look like this:

Would substitution or elimination be more effective in solving this system? Why?
$2x - y = 5$
$x + 2y = 15$

It is not necessary to work out the whole solution to think about this question. Instead, it asks students to think about the initial steps of these two approaches, giving students a chance to practice making the initial strategy choice. This is what makes it "part-task."

I like this question, and I think it would be a good follow-up to the case comparison. I think the case comparison is a better way to introduce the choice between elimination and substitution, but this practice question could be a good way to follow-up on it.

TECHNIQUE 5: MISTAKE ANALYSIS
In addition to all the above, I also ask students to analyze incorrect solutions. Here is an incorrect example that I share with students from the Algebra by Example project:[56]

---

56. Algebra by Example (SERP Institute): https://www.serpinstitute.org/algebra-by-example

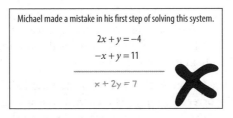

Julie Booth – co-creator of the Algebra by Example project – studied whether students benefit from studying not just correct examples but also incorrect ones.[57] This was a true random experiment, performed with students who were studying algebra with the Cognitive Tutor learning software. Some students received the typical mix of worked examples, self-explanation prompts, and practice that the software provides. Other students were randomly assigned to receive incorrect examples as part of their studies. Booth found benefits to these incorrect examples.

I run incorrect worked examples exactly as I present correct ones. I use the same routines as I described earlier in the book (Chapter 3). The self-explanation prompts should draw attention to the error and ask students to explain it. The practice problem at the end should be similar enough to the incorrect solution that students have the chance to practice avoiding that same error.

Michael made a mistake in his first step of solving this system. $2x + y = -4$ $-x + y = 11$ $x + 2y = 7$ ✗	Michael should have subtracted first. If he had done that he would have $3x = -15$. Why would that get him closer to the solution?	**Your turn** Solve the system: $x + 3y = 14$ $x + y = 6$

Why would it benefit students to study incorrect examples, as opposed to studying equivalent correct ones? Booth suggests two benefits:

- It helps students learn that such an approach is wrong, so they don't continue to use it.
- It helps students understand why it is wrong, which deepens understanding.

57. Booth, J. L., Lange, K. E., Koedinger, K. R., & Newton, K. J. (2013) "Using example problems to improve student learning in algebra: Differentiating between correct and incorrect examples," *Learning and Instruction*, 25, 24–34.

This is why the researchers clearly mark the example as "incorrect." The main benefits come from explaining *why* a wrong idea isn't correct, not from discovering the error. (Though if students can easily spot the error, there's no harm in challenging them to spot it on their own.)

From experience, I recommend that you follow the model of these researchers and clearly mark incorrect examples as incorrect. Use a large red "X" to make sure students know that the answer is wrong. Don't ask students to guess whether it's right or wrong. It can only lead to tears and frustration.

Early in my career I had an enthusiasm for the mistakes that students make while doing math. I started collecting them and cataloging them. I created a website focused entirely on this work, called mathmistakes.org. It was only natural that I would try to turn these student mistakes into a learning activity for my students. But I made a big mistake myself, and it soured me on using mistakes in the classroom for the longest time.

When I presented a mistake to my students in class, I wouldn't tell them it was incorrect. Instead, I would ask them to debate: is this correct or not? Looking back, this was a significant error on my own part. Do you have any idea how frustrating it is to listen to students desperately defend a wrong answer in a classroom debate? And students would only grow more frustrated when I took the opposite side of the debate, as I had to – I couldn't let them leave class thinking the wrong approach was actually the correct one! I soon stopped using mistakes in class at all.

There is, perhaps, a role to play for "Is this wrong?" activities in class. But not until very late in the unit. The key to learning from mistakes is being able to *recognize that they are mistakes and explain why*. Until students are ready to do that, they shouldn't be asked to guess. Students will take the bait and put the teacher in a difficult situation.

In general, mistake analysis works only when students have some experience solving the problem correctly. It is useful to use towards the middle of a unit, just as students are starting to become more independent in their problem solving. Mistake analysis gives you a chance to help students learn to recognize common errors before they become habit.

All of the ideas in this chapter should challenge the belief that practice should solely come from solving problems.

It's true that studying complete worked examples is often most useful towards the start of the unit. (Though they're also useful as feedback; see Chapter 6.) But I hope you're seeing that you can do a lot with worked-out solutions. You can knock out lines from them and turn them into completion problems. You can take a pair of them and ask students to compare them. And you can write a wrong solution and ask students to analyze that.

Worked examples and problem solving are equal partners in learning. You can't get very far with one without the other, and some of the strongest practice formats neatly integrate the two. Studying solutions and solving problems are two ingredients that go great together. When both are on the table, a lot of learning happens.

IN SHORT

- **Whole-task practice** preserves the overall context of the skill, even as it focuses students on specific elements of the skill. **Part-task practice** focuses only on those specific elements. **Both forms of practice are important** in developing expertise, particularly as tasks grow more complex.
- Before studying an example, it can sometimes be useful to work on a "**meaning-making problem**" whose purpose is to teach students what the problem means and what its solutions look like.
- **Completion problems** remove steps from a worked example and ask students to fill in the missing steps on their own. This is a type of practice that combines the benefits of problem solving and worked examples. When the steps are removed systematically over several problems, this is called "fading."
- Two other useful practice formats that use worked-out solutions are **case comparisons** and **mistake analysis**. These techniques are particularly useful towards the end of a learning sequence.

CHAPTER 6: GIVING WORKED EXAMPLES AS FEEDBACK

In this chapter I'll make the case that you can use worked examples as feedback. But before I can do that, we need to clear up what exactly feedback is and how it works. Well, maybe we can't clear those things up entirely – that would be a whole other book! But there are some simple things we can say about how feedback might help learning.

A SIMPLE THEORY OF FEEDBACK

When someone tells you they "gave feedback" it could mean a lot of different things. A teacher gives feedback when she agrees with something a student said. She's also giving feedback when she grades a set of exams. A supervisor might "give some constructive feedback," which is code for voicing criticism. And a computer can give feedback when it automatically reports to a student that their answer is incorrect.

Despite the range of meanings, when people talk about "giving feedback" they usually mean something fitting a core set of qualities:

- It is in response to something a student did or said.
- It is presented to each individual student separately.
- It evaluates what the student did or said.
- It is almost always a written or spoken comment.

Think of comments on a paper or a one-on-one conference to review a test – that's conventional feedback.

Feedback is widely thought to be important for learning. And it really would be quite difficult to learn anything hard without getting any feedback at all. But in a famous review of the research literature, Kluger and DeNisi found that over a third of experimental tests of feedback actually *harmed* student learning.[58] A decade later, Shute performed another influential review of research on feedback, and characterized this body of work as "inconsistent, contradictory,

---

58. Kluger, A. N., & DeNisi, A. (1996) "The effects of feedback interventions on performance: A historical review, a meta-analysis, and a preliminary feedback intervention theory," *Psychological Bulletin*, 119 (2), 254.

and highly variable."[59] That's not great news for feedback research. But it doesn't mean that research has nothing to tell us about feedback; research is telling us that conventional feedback often doesn't work.

Given how complicated the research picture can get, I propose that we go back to the basics. Suppose a student says or does something, and then a teacher responds. How could that response possibly help the student's learning? There really are just two ways:

- the response could teach that student something new, OR
- the response could motivate that student to learn something new on their own.

And that's it, because feedback isn't magic. If it helps students, it has to be via one of these two routes.

Suppose you have just given your class a quiz. While marking the quiz, it becomes clear that many students had issues with the third question, the one about adding fractions. You carefully mark each solution with a check or an "X" while scrawling comments in the margins, things like "Did you mean to multiply?" or "Close!" or "See me."

Is this motivating? Is it effective teaching? Conventional feedback often has a hard time standing up to these basic questions.

I prefer, whenever possible, to give feedback *in the form of a learning activity*. I customize these activities in response to the issues I see in my students' work. By using learning activities that I know to be motivating and instructive, I end up with more confidence that they're actually helping. But it's important to note that "feedback as a learning activity" looks a bit different than what is conventionally considered to be "giving feedback":

- Instead of being presented to each individual student, it is typically presented to the whole group.
- Instead of responding to student work via written or spoken comments, it responds with a classroom activity. The classroom activity should not be passive – it should require the student to actively think about something that will help their understanding.
- Instead of focusing attention on the student's work, it focuses on ideas that students need more help with (as indicated by their work).

---

59. Shute, V. J. (2007) "Focus on formative feedback," *ETS Research Report Series*, 2007 (1), i–47.

Don't be fooled by these surface-level differences. All you're doing is teaching, but teaching in response to your students is the best form of feedback.

A WORKED EXAMPLE FEEDBACK ROUTINE

To give feedback in this way, we need to scour our students' work for ideas they need to better understand. We want to look carefully at the mistakes they've made and understand how we might address them. Then, we need to put together some sort of activity that addresses just the need that we have identified. What we need most of all are sturdy teaching tools that can be customized to reflect just what the students need to study.

A worked example routine fits this bill exactly. It's customizable, motivating and productive for learning. While many other learning activities also work well, I love creating worked examples for feedback. It forces me to think very carefully about precisely what it is that I think students need most to learn, and the result is a tool that can directly address that need. It does exactly what I want feedback to do.

Conventional feedback still plays a role for me. I mark quizzes and tests and return them to students; I'm not some kind of monster. But learning activities are the element of feedback that I think does the most.

I have a routine I try to follow that combines conventional feedback, worked examples, practice and revision all in a neat tidy package. Suppose that students have taken a quiz or some other kind of assessment. Here's what I'll do:

1. **Mark it:** I mark the assessments with very simple marks, checks and "X"s.
2. **Focus on just one problem:** I look through student work and try to find a single type of problem that my students would gain the most from studying.
3. **Create a worked example:** I create an example-problem pair for class, then run the activity in class (or assign it for homework, if in a time crunch).
4. **Call for revision:** Then, after the activity, I return the quizzes to students in class. I ask them to revise any incorrect answers in class, and to start the next activity when they are finished.

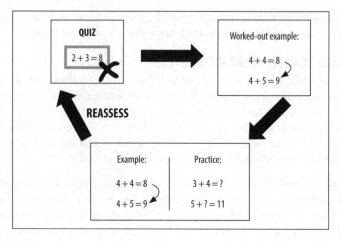

That's the big-picture view of my feedback routine. Now, let's go through it step by step.

STAGE 1: MARK IT

It is my view that marking on its own is a poor form of feedback. This follows from the simple view on feedback that I shared above. Does marking motivate students to learn more? Does it teach them anything? Well, very often it teaches students that they are wrong. And it motivates them to get emotional, demanding an explanation. Maybe we shouldn't mark at all.

I do mark my students' work for correctness, even when there is no grade attached – though far less often than many other teachers do. I don't think it leads to much learning, but I do think it is a tangible way of showing students that their work is important to me and I am reading it with care. Besides, it's pretty much expected for teachers to mark quizzes and tests, and sometimes it pays to meet expectations.

Marking is also a natural way to start gathering information about how students are thinking about the material. Where do they seem to have confidence? Where are the areas for growth? Marking for correctness can be tedious, but it's a disciplined way to pick up on details.

The final reason why I always begin by marking is for the sake of revision. At the very end of this routine, I will ask students to improve their work. I have found that without clear right/wrong indications, nearly every student will assume their work is basically correct! Revision is valuable, so I take the time to make sure students know they have definitely made an error.

Though I do begin by marking, I don't think of it as the main source of feedback. That is to come through the learning activity in Stage 3.

STAGES 2 & 3: FOCUS ON A PROBLEM; CREATE A WORKED EXAMPLE

There's only so much you can teach in one lesson; for that reason, in my feedback I want to focus on just one problem to help my students with. Maybe two, but that's already pushing it.

When I say, "focus on just one problem," what I really mean is to describe, as specifically as possible, what type of problem it is that students are struggling with. I'll give an example from my geometry class. After teaching the Pythagorean theorem, I gave the class a short quiz. The quiz gave students a variety of right triangles and asked them to find the missing side. No big deal; I figured everyone would ace it.

When I got the quizzes back, my hopes were crushed. But I was also intrigued. My students only had trouble with some of the triangles. With others, their answers were entirely accurate. Here is one of the quizzes from that class, from my student Laura; can you spot her issue?

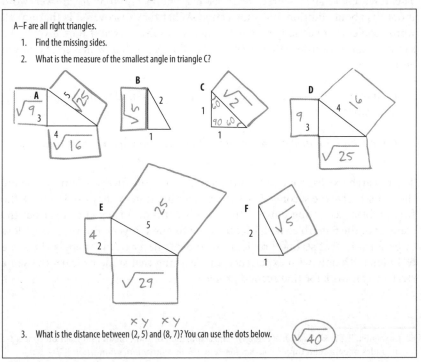

Look carefully, and you'll see that Laura got every question right when the triangle had a *missing hypotenuse*. In contrast, she made a mistake on every single problem with a *missing leg*. Many of the students in my class made the same error that Laura did. Experienced geometry teachers will recognize this mistake – it's a Hall of Famer, a classic in the oeuvre of student math mistakes.

This is what I mean by trying to get as specific as possible. It would be easy to say that Laura and her classmates were struggling with "Pythagorean theorem problems." That's not specific enough, though. What they're struggling with are *"Missing-leg Pythagorean theorem problems."* They already know how to solve half the problems we need to teach; our learning activity can help them with the other half.

Teachers need to appreciate this. When you're learning something new, often the tiniest changes can transform a problem from "I can do this" to "this is impossible." What students are struggling with is often just a specific branch of a skill, not the entire skill itself.

One of my favorite sources for this idea is Carpenter and Moser's 1984 paper.[60] The researchers spent three years asking young children to answer word problems about addition and subtraction. What they discovered is that not all word problems are equally easy for students to solve – even if they involve the same numbers. Consider these two word problems, both of which can be solved with 13 – 5:

> *Connie had 13 marbles. She gave 5 of them to Jim. How many does she have now?*

> *Connie had 5 marbles. She wants to have 13. How many more does she need?*

The researchers observed that students could solve the first problem well before they could solve the second. The issue is that the strategy they used to solve the first problem (counting down 5 from 13) is natural, since you can act out the transfer of the 5 marbles with objects, or with one's fingers. But there is no loss to perform in that second problem, so students never think to apply the same technique. It's only with experience and learning that students learn the same strategy can work for that second problem.

---

60. Carpenter, T. P., & Moser, J. M. (1984) "The acquisition of addition and subtraction concepts in grades one through three," *Journal for Research in Mathematics Education*, 179–202.

The case I make for focusing on one problem – or even one specific *branch* of a problem – is that this is often the source of student mistakes. It's not a weak understanding of a skill; it's that they have firm understanding of one sub-skill and a weak understanding of another. We can help them by explicitly teaching that other sub-skill through a worked example (or some other learning activity).

In the case of Laura's geometry class, I created a worked example that took for granted that she knew how to solve a missing-hypotenuse version of the problem. What she and others needed to learn was the missing-leg version, which I presented in a solution:

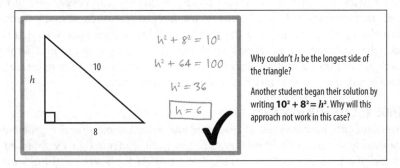

Why couldn't h be the longest side of the triangle?

Another student began their solution by writing $10^2 + 8^2 = h^2$. Why will this approach not work in this case?

Note that the explanation prompts focus attention entirely on Laura's mistake. This is just the learning that Laura and her classmates needed. I presented the problem and questions using the routine I described in Chapter 3. To wrap up, I asked students to try to solve two problems on their own, making sure they could avoid the mistake so many of them had made on their quizzes:

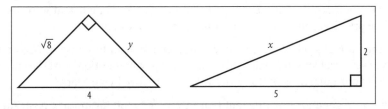

This obviously takes time, but it's time well spent.

The focus on just one problem is often a sticking point when I explain to others how I give feedback. The issue is that quizzes and tests often contain many different errors, often committed by entirely different students. If a teacher gives a ten-question test, there may be five different problems that students need to improve on. How do you choose just one of them?

My own answer to this question is: you can't. This is an issue with longer exams, and a reason not to give them. As educator Harry Fletcher-Wood once wrote as a comment on my blog, to give good feedback you have to "design a test with the feedback in mind."[61] My school allows me to choose how to assess my students, and I choose to only give short quizzes. Trust me, the students don't mind either.

There are some workarounds that bend the "focus on one problem" rule. First, you can share more than one worked example per class. (You could skip the self-explanation prompts to cut down on time.) Second, you can stretch out the feedback over one or two class periods, so that you can cover more of the issues that students had. A last idea is you can try to give students many worked examples to study at once on a sheet. When I did this, I designed it so that the examples matched the questions on the quiz: "If you got question 3 wrong, check out example 3 on the handout." But it took quite some work to create all those examples, and I've only rarely done this in practice.

STAGE 4: CALL FOR REVISION

After students have studied an example and solved some practice problems, I am ready to return their marked quizzes. I tell students that I've marked a "check" if a problem is 100% correct, and an "X" if there was anything wrong with it. I do this because I like giving students the challenge of finding their mistake, and I dislike the tedium of circling precisely what is wrong in every student's solution.

This is the part where I say something encouraging. "There were a lot of mistakes on question 2," I'll say, "but we just studied an example that showed how to approach it accurately. If you understood the example and were able to do the practice, you now know how to approach question 2."

I'll then direct students to that question and ask them to revise it. "Correctly solve every problem that had a mistake, starting with question 2. At the end, I'll collect your quizzes again to see how you've improved your work."

Revision is good for learning, but I also think it's good for morale. Assessment is an emotional experience. It can feel like you're being judged, and I have no doubt this is part of the reason so many experimental studies on feedback seem to backfire – a lot of feedback makes people feel bad. Nobody wants to feel like they've failed at a task that they can't overcome. Revision is a chance for everyone to feel as if they are up to the task. This math is not too much.

---

61. Fletcher-Wood, H. (2017) Comment on "Teaching, in General": https://problemproblems. wordpress.com/2017/11/15/teaching-in-general/

That's the message I want students to get from my feedback, and it's why I end the routine with revision.

Worked examples can be useful feedback even outside of this routine, I've found. If a student has a mistake that doesn't merit focus during a full-class activity, I sometimes scrawl short little examples in the margins. That way, the student has something to refer to while revising their work.

This can get cumbersome if you have to do it often, but you can just as well scrawl the example on the board for anyone who needs to see it.

The other context in which worked examples make for great feedback is online problem solving. A few years ago I learned about a math practice website called DeltaMath. I decided to try it out with one of my algebra classes, expecting the class to whine and moan about how boring it was to repeatedly practice algebra problems.

They loved it. The class asked if I could assign it for homework, which I enthusiastically (but cautiously) did. Even more surprising, parents started reaching out to me, to thank me for using the math practice website. The website is dead simple – it asks questions, tells you if they're right or wrong, and then gives you another. What was going on?

I am writing this chapter while sheltering in place at home during the coronavirus pandemic in 2020. Like other teachers, the last several months were a crash course in online learning. When I asked students at the end of this pandemic year what they liked most about our online experience – surprise, surprise – DeltaMath came up often. But when I asked *what* they liked about it, a theory of mine was confirmed: the worked examples are key. "I liked that if you didn't understand something, it had examples to show you," one student wrote. This sentiment was echoed by a majority of students. Not every student raved, but those who did liked the clear examples that followed-up on wrong answers.

People don't like feeling hopeless, and many people experience math as a hopeless venture. Feedback is extraordinarily complicated in some ways, but in others it's a very simple game. When you tell someone they've done something wrong, you take away hope. When you teach them how to do it right, you give it back. That's what feedback can do.

IN SHORT

- Feedback is not magic, and quite often it fails to help students. **Feedback only helps students when it teaches or motivates** them to learn what they do not yet know.
- I use **students' mistakes as inspiration for worked examples**. The worked examples focus on precisely the type of problem that students most need to learn.
- This works best with **focused assessments** such as short quizzes. The technique can be adapted for feedback on longer tests, but it is more difficult to find one thing to focus on.
- Once students have studied the correct solution, I ask them to **revise** their mistaken work. Students often find it empowering to see concrete evidence of their own growth.

CHAPTER 7: DESIGNING WORKED EXAMPLES

Here is an example that I like very much from the Algebra by Example project:

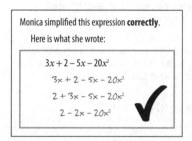

Monica simplified this expression **correctly**.
Here is what she wrote:

$$3x + 2 - 5x - 20x^2$$
$$3x + 2 - 5x - 20x^2$$
$$2 + 3x - 5x - 20x^2$$
$$2 - 2x - 20x^2$$

There are elements of its design that even someone who has never taught mathematics before could admire. The example clearly indicates that the solution is correct, letting students know there is something to learn from it. And unlike a typical textbook example, this solution is concise. There is no explanatory commentary running along the side.

Someone with experience teaching algebra might notice more:

- Whoever chose the problem chose wisely. Students have a hard time combining like terms, especially when the like terms ("$3x$" and "$-5x$") aren't next to each other. This problem was inspired by a common pitfall, and shows students a way to veer around it.
- The strategy the solution shows – using the commutative ("order doesn't matter") property of addition – is one of those little things that students who are good at algebra just "naturally" do. By making the move explicit, the entire class has a chance to add it to their mathematical toolkit.

It is a well-crafted example and pedagogically on-target. It is ready for use in the classroom.

Most textbook examples don't meet this standard. Contrast the above example with this next one, which I find unnecessarily confusing:

Algorithm for adding numbers

Step 1: Stack the number so that each number is lined up according to its place value.

$$\begin{array}{r} 87 \\ + 65 \\ \hline \end{array}$$

Step 2: Add the digits at the ones place. Since $5 + 7 = 12$, write "2" **below** the line and "1" (that means "10") **above** the numbers in the tens place.

$$\begin{array}{r} 1 \\ 87 \\ + 65 \\ \hline 2 \end{array}$$

Step 3: Almost done! Now add the digits in the tens place. Since $1 + 8 + 6 = 15$, place a 5 below (that means "50") and place 1 **to the left** in the hundreds place (that means "100").

$$\begin{array}{r} 1 \\ 87 \\ + 65 \\ \hline 152 \end{array}$$

The final answer is $100 + 50 + 2 =$ **152**.

It's a shame, because if you were to strip the text away entirely you'd be left with a pretty good example:

- It uses different fonts to clearly distinguish between the statement of the problem and the student's solution. This makes it clear which part of the work students should seek to emulate themselves.
- It separates steps of a procedure into clearly distinctive chunks, much like a series of cartoon panels. It gives instructions in stages, like the LEGO booklets that my children love.
- It is a good problem to show the solution to. 87 + 65 avoids unnecessary repetition of digits; a problem like 66 + 44 would be somewhat more difficult for students to follow, as some of the steps and digits would repeat and mush together. Working-memory researchers have found that when someone tries to remember similar items, they can get confused when they try to recall them. See for instance the evidence reviewed in Oberauer et al. (2016).[62] I know of no study that attempts to measure this, but I bet this explains why it's harder to learn from problems such as 66 + 44.

This fairly typical textbook example could become much more accessible to students by simply cutting away all of the words.

---

62. Oberauer, K., Farrell, S., Jarrold, C., & Lewandowsky, S. (2016) "What limits working memory capacity?," *Psychological Bulletin*, 142 (7), 758.

Designing worked examples is both an art and a science. The art comes from experience, especially knowing what sorts of problems students tend to struggle with. We can't show examples that will cover every possible case, so we design examples that will evoke some of the most common difficulties.

The science comes from research psychologists and cognitive scientists. Researchers have compared worked examples through experiments, noting which ones were easier for students to learn from. The result is a collection of helpful principles to keep in mind while creating a worked-out solution.

I'll begin by briefly describing the art of choosing good problems for worked examples, before moving on to the science.

CHOOSING PROBLEMS FOR EXAMPLES

How do you choose a problem for a worked example? In their piece "A Worked Example for Creating Worked Examples," authors McGinn, Lange and Booth suggest we start with mistakes:

> Think about past mistakes you have seen students make while solving problems associated with the objective. Choose one misconception or error for each example. The goal is to focus students' attention on one aspect of the problem at a time.[63]

That is, thinking about particular mistakes can guide us towards a learning goal. Mistakes tell us what students need to learn – we can use them to guide the creation of worked examples.

There are formal and informal ways to do this. Of course, as experience piles up a teacher will remember which mistakes their students most often make. There are various ways to supplement this store of knowledge. One way is to assign students a few problems at the start of the unit to see what mistakes arise. Other math teachers often have pointed thoughts about which problems tend to be the trickiest for students; this can make a good topic for teachers to discuss at departmental meetings. There are also collections of common mistakes that teachers can research – my own website mathmistakes.org contains many different mistakes, most of them waiting patiently for a teacher to turn them into a learning activity.

---

63. McGinn, K. M., Lange, K. E., & Booth, J. L. (2015) "A worked example for creating worked examples," *Mathematics Teaching in the Middle School*, 21 (1), 26–33.

THE SCIENCE OF EXAMPLE DESIGN

Once you choose a problem, next comes creating a solution. The challenge is to create a solution that students will be able to learn from studying. As luck would have it, research psychologists and cognitive scientists have been studying for decades how to design these effectively.

Mayer and Moreno's 2003 paper contains a handy summary of the evidence.[64] Whether students are looking at a whiteboard, website, video, graph, image, slides or a worked example, there is a tendency to experience cognitive overload during their attempt at learning. There is often just too much presented to a student to allow them to focus on learning something new. Designers of learning materials need to be sensitive to the potential for overload without reducing whatever complexity is intrinsic to the topic itself.

Mayer lists helpful design principles for managing this kind of cognitive overload. The ones most relevant to the design of mathematical materials are:

1. **Cut stuff:** Ruthlessly exclude information from materials that doesn't pertain to the content; even interesting facts, trivia or tidbits can distract students from the main mathematical idea. Give those non-essentials the boot, especially when the content gets complex.

2. **Eliminate redundancy:** If students can access the idea one way, don't distract by providing it in a second way. Written text is usually the main culprit of redundancy. Often, as in the addition example at the start of this chapter, it's text that has got to go.

3. **Off-load explanation from the solution:** If some explanation is truly necessary to make sense of the material, don't try to stuff it into the solution. It's better to just describe it verbally while displaying the solution. (The brain has different channels for taking in information; it's best to spread information across those channels. Mayer calls this the "multimedia effect.")

4. **Align words with images:** If labels or annotations are truly necessary for making sense of the material, try to integrate them into the solution. By placing them below or to the side of a solution on the page we force students to split their attention between two visual fields. That forces students to remember what is in one while they race back to the other, which taxes working-memory resources unnecessarily.

---

64. Mayer, R. E., & Moreno, R. (2003) "Nine ways to reduce cognitive load in multimedia learning," *Educational Psychologist*, 38 (1), 43–52.

5. **Preview the structure:** If a solution is complex, structure it for students. Break it into little chunks and label each one (e.g. "Solve for x" or "Substitute"). Before showing the full example, you can run through the chunks of the proof: "First we're going to solve for x, then we're going to perform substitution..." That lets students stay organized while keeping track of all the details in the example.
6. **Segmenting:** If the solution to a problem is long, consider chunking it up and studying the pieces one at a time.

My own use of examples improved once I learned to pay attention to these techniques while designing solutions. There are often subtle ways to improve the legibility of the solution that make an immense difference in class.

The first three of these principles relate to *reducing* the information presented in the example (weeding, avoiding redundancy, off-loading). The fourth principle relates to *integrating* the words with the mathematics in an example (aligning words with diagrams or equations). The last two principles relate to *structuring* a complex solution (previewing, segmenting).

I've already shown the benefits of reducing information at the start of this chapter. The "combining like terms" example used only mathematical expressions to convey the mathematical idea. It would have added nothing to include a detailed explanation in the example itself – the teacher can provide that in class, if needed. And the confusing textbook addition example was immediately improved when we deleted all the text on the left.

It's not always possible, but I always aim for my worked examples to be entirely *wordless*. Words have to earn their way into a solution.

Sometimes, though, words really are necessary. In that case, the suggestion of research is to try to combine the words with the diagram as closely as is possible.

Some of the best word/math integration that I've seen comes from the Play With Your Math project by math teachers Joey Kelly and Xi Yu. Their website consists of a collection of playful, open-ended math problems. But posing those problems inevitably involves sharing some brief mathematical explanations. Look how thoughtfully words, numbers and symbols are combined in their presentation of the "Persistence" problem:[65]

---

65. Egendorf, A., & Starkshall, G. "Persistence," Play With Your Math: https://playwithyourmath. com/2019/12/02/22-persistence/

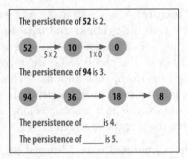

There is much to appreciate in this bit of mathematical exposition:

- The diagram contains the main mathematical idea, and the arrows are a clean visual metaphor to represent the abstract notion of carrying out a step in the process.
- The top flowchart in the diagram is extremely explicit. But notice that the next flowchart contains a bit less information – this time the multiplication below each arrow has been removed. After that comes the problem. Reading this problem feels, to me, like having my hand held by a comforting teacher, leading me right into the middle of a terrific and complex set-up for a fascinating problem.
- Words are used sparingly, and they are put right beside the flowcharts. You can take in both the flowcharts and the sentences in the same visual field – they are entirely integrated. There is no need to shift from one side of the page to the other.

The power of the integration principle is clearest in its violation. Consider this set of problematic instructions I created for Marilyn Burns' multiplication game "Circles and Stars.": [66]

66. Burns, M. (2007). *About Teaching Mathematics: A K-8 Resource*. Math Solutions Publications.

Roll the first die.	
Draw that many circles.	
Roll the second die.	
Draw that many stars in each circle.	
Record the total number of stars. Switch players. Whoever has the most points after 8 rounds wins.	**Total:** 10

This pushes the written instructions to the left side. It's necessary to move your sight from left to right on the page to make sense of the rules of the game.

Contrast it with this set of instructions, which does a wonderful job at combining necessary words into the diagram in a clean way:

Rol the first die and draw that many circles.	Roll the second die and draw that many stars in each circle.	Record the total number of stars.
		Total: 10
		Switch players. Whoever has the most points after 8 rounds wins.

Split attention is a powerful effect. Good examples are designed with an eye on how to minimize it.

STRUCTURING A LONG SOLUTION

There are some very complex procedures that students sometimes need to learn. If you try to present these procedures through a worked example (not a bad idea) it often requires students to study an extremely long solution (a bad idea).

Here, for instance, is a perfectly reasonable attempt at creating a solution for students to study. The problem is to solve a system of equations where one equation describes a line and the other a circle:

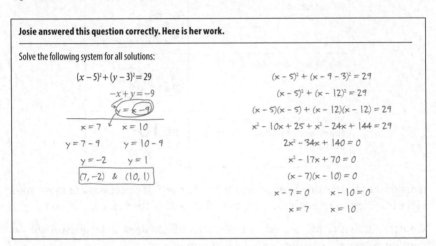

The solution is fine; the problem is its length. Students will be unlikely to take this all in at once, and many will be scared off and completely unmotivated to dig into the long string of unstructured symbols. We need a way to rein this one in.

Richard Catrambone is another researcher whose ideas are worth mining. In a 1998 paper he provided evidence that students gain more from studying complex solutions that have grouped steps into sub-goals and meaningfully labeled them.[67] This does introduce some text to the worked example, but in this case it's worth it. Here is a redesign of the above solution that groups and labels the sub-goals:

---

67. Catrambone, R. (1998) "The subgoal learning model: Creating better examples so that students can solve novel problems," *Journal of Experimental Psychology: General*, 127 (4), 355.

Solve the following system for all solutions:

$$(x-5)^2 + (y-3)^2 = 29$$
$$-x+y = -9$$

1. Solve for a variable

$$-x+y=-9$$
$$y = x - 9$$

2. Substitute and expand

$$(x-5)^2 + (x-9-3)^2 = 29$$
$$(x-5)^2 + (x-12)^2 = 29$$
$$(x-5)(x-5) + (x-12)(x-12) = 29$$
$$x^2 - 10x + 25 + x^2 - 24x + 144 = 29$$

3. Solve the quadratic

$$2x^2 - 34x + 140 = 0$$
$$x^2 - 17x + 70 = 0$$
$$(x-7)(x-10) = 0$$
$$x - 7 = 0 \qquad x - 10 = 0$$
$$x = 7 \qquad x = 10$$

4. Find both coordinates

$$x = 7 \qquad x = 10$$
$$y = 7 - 9 \qquad y = 10 - 9$$
$$y = -2 \qquad y = 1$$
$$(7, -2) \quad \& \quad (10, 1)$$

Admittedly, this is still a lengthy procedure. I could imagine it being quite difficult for students to take in all at once. Following the advice of Mayer (2003), we might **preview** the sub-goals for students before showing any of the details. ("The first step is going to be solving for a variable, and then we're going to substitute and expand...") This might familiarize them with the overall strategy before filling in the details, making it easier to learn from studying the solution.

Alternatively, we could decide to only teach part of the procedure at once. One way of doing this is to only give students a **snapshot** of the solution. That is, instead of saying, "let's analyze Simon's solution" you would say, "let's see how Simon began his solution." Here is what that might look like:

> **Solve the following system for all solutions:**
>
> $$(x-5)^2 + (y-3)^2 = 29$$
>
> $$-x+y=-9$$
>
> Here were Simon's first two steps:
>
> $$-x+y=-9$$
>
> $$y = x - 9$$
>
> $$(x-5)^2 + (y-3)^2 = 29$$
>
> $$(x-5)^2 + (x-9-3)^2 = 29$$
>
> Analyze each step and explain what Simon did.
>
> Bonus: Can you complete his work?

We can include as much or as little of the solution in our snapshot as we want. We can start with just the first few steps, and slowly build up.

Here is how Clara began her solution to this system of equations:	Your turn:
$$(x-5)^2 + (y-3)^2 = 29$$ $$-x+y=-9$$	$$(x+4)^2 + y^2 = 10$$ $$x-2y=-9$$
1. Solve for a variable	
$$-x+y=-9$$ $$y = x - 9$$	
2. Substitute and expand	
$$(x-5)^2 + (y-3)^2 = 29$$ $$(x-5)^2 + (x-9-3)^2 = 29$$ $$(x-5)^2 + (x-12)^2 = 29$$ $$(x-5)(x-5)+(x-12)(x-12) = 29$$ $$x^2 - 10x + 25 + x^2 - 24x + 144 = 29$$	
3. Simplify	
$$2x^2 - 34x + 140 = 0$$	

It takes time to grow more comfortable designing materials that reflect these principles. The good news, though, is that it's not just about worked examples. The design principles are about designing useful mathematical materials, *period*. It's just as much about worksheets, problem sets, game instructions, slides or the blackboard as it is about worked examples.

Math itself is messy. It sprawls across the page in unexpected ways. It gets crossed out and evolves during the process of thinking about a problem.

The materials that students learn best from, though, are the opposite: clean, organized, and thoughtfully structured. This is an ideal that I often fail to reach, but always strive for.

IN SHORT

- When **choosing** a problem for a worked example, look towards a problem students often make mistakes on.
- Research suggests three ways teachers can improve their worked examples: by **reducing unnecessary information** (often text); by **integrating diagrams with words** (if the words are truly necessary); by **structuring and labeling** complex solutions.
- When it comes to long solutions, it can also be helpful to break it up into smaller "**snapshots**" that focus on only part of a solution at a time.

CHAPTER 8: TEACHING PROOF WITH EXAMPLES

Are worked examples only useful for teaching simple ideas? I don't think so, but based on the previous chapters I can see how you might think that. Most of the examples I've shared are for teaching relatively short procedures. In doing so, perhaps I've given you the wrong idea. In this last chapter, I'll try to correct any misconceptions – examples *can* help teach complex mathematics.

Geometric proof is the least algorithmic of the skills I teach. It's also one of the hardest. One school of thought is that learning proof is hard because students are asked to justify boring theorems using unnecessarily formal and precise language. (This is often true.) Another thought is that writing geometry proof is simply complex by nature. To write a proof successfully, students need to explore a diagram, remember the goal, and use everything they've already learned in class to solve a logical puzzle, all of which is just plain *hard*. (This is also true.) Many teachers and schools have decided it's not worth the hassle and moved away from teaching proof entirely. Which is a shame, I think, because proof is beautiful. There aren't many places left in the curriculum for creative, visual thinking. Geometry proof is still hanging on, but it's increasingly an endangered species of school mathematics.

Worked examples are not easy to adapt for teaching proof. Reiss and Renkl point out that the finished product of a proof gives you little insight into how the prover created it:

> A "traditional" worked-out example of a proof would contain the statement to be proved and the sequence of solution steps as a kind of ideal solution process. However, such an "ideal" solution process of a mathematical proof does not reflect the real solution process, even not that of an expert. It simply displays a type of an end product of a proving process.[68]

We could show students completed proofs, but that would be like simply telling students that 5 times 19 is 95. It would also be like handing students a lovely

---

68. Reiss, K., & Renkl, A. (2002) "Learning to prove: The idea of heuristic examples,"*ZDM*, 34 (1), 29–35.

paragraph and asking them to create their own work of similar quality. These are ideal end-products – they leave the process of creating the solution entirely hidden. Students need more.

The approach presented by Reiss and Renkl was to develop a new format they call "heuristic worked examples." These examples use fictional student dialogue to present the process of discovering a proof. Here's a sample of that dialogue:

Nina and Tom have drawn and measured parallelograms. In doing so, they noticed that opposing sides were always of equal length. Moreover, opposing angles were always of equal size.

Tom: "We measured so many parallelograms: We have drawn all kinds of quadrangles and always we recognized that the opposing sides were of equal length and opposing angles were of equal size. I think, it has to be like this!"

Nina: "I think you are right, but I don't know a reason. Maybe by chance, we have only drawn parallelograms for which the statement is correct? We cannot measure the angles and sides exactly. Perhaps they were only approximately of the same size."

Tom: "So let's try to prove our assumption like mathematicians would do!"[69]

The heuristic worked example continues like this as Nina and Tom prove their conjecture.

Their approach is intriguing, though not one I would use. (Their examples are lengthy and quite difficult to make and use, in my view.) Still, I think any approach to using examples to teach proof needs to tangle with the difficulties they point to. If we *are* going to use completed proofs to teach the process of creating a proof, how do we uncover the *process* of creating them?

Earlier in this book, I argued that learning from worked examples works when we **analyze** the solution, **explain** its finer points, and **apply** the solution to a new problem. To be prepared to learn from the worked example, students often need to **notice** and **remember** information before studying the solution (Chapter 1). Those principles are still true – we might need to tweak the routine to accommodate the complexity of proof, but we wouldn't want to give up on these fundamental elements of learning from examples.

In this chapter, I'll explain how I adapt the principles of teaching with examples for geometry proof. The main shifts that I make are these:

- **Start with a goal-free problem:** To make sense of a proof, there is a lot to notice in a diagram and remember from earlier studies. To help students notice and remember all this info, I often begin the class

---

69. Reiss, K. M., Heinze, A., Renkl, A., & Groß, C. (2008) "Reasoning and proof in geometry: Effects of a learning environment based on heuristic worked-out examples," *ZDM*, 40 (3), 455–467.

with a problem that has **non-specific goals** (sometimes called "goal-free" problems).

- **Preview the structure:** Proofs are often long and wordy, so I **preview** the structure of the proof and **segment** the proof into meaningful sections (using the ideas of Chapter 7).

- **I think aloud, you analyze:** I present a complete and correct proof to my students, but the complete proof doesn't show the *process* of creating it. Even though I usually ask students to study an example on their own, in this case I explain the process of creating the proof, annotating the diagram as I go (often called "**modeling**").

- **Lots of whole-task practice:** So much goes into successfully writing a proof that I rely even more on the whole-task practice formats that I described in Chapter 5. I especially increase my use of **completion problems, mistake analysis, fading** and other similar practice techniques.

These are a lot of shifts! But the underlying principles behind this approach to teaching haven't changed. It's only how they appear on the surface that's different. I'll explain those differences in the context of a proof that I might teach in my high-school geometry class. We would do this towards the middle of the course, after having practiced and grown confident in using angle theorems and in identifying congruent triangles. The class is then ready to begin writing more complex geometric arguments – which is the focus of this chapter. And while I'll focus on geometry proof, I think these same shifts could help us teach other kinds of proof or problem solving.

START WITH A GOAL-FREE PROBLEM

Here is a diagram:

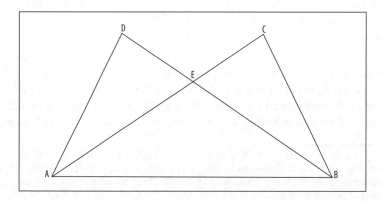

It contains overlapping triangles. Can you see triangles ABC and BAD? I'll tell you that they are **congruent** – if you wanted to, you could cover one of those triangles perfectly with the other (as long as flipping is allowed). This is given information.

Now, given that those triangles are congruent, what else is congruent in this diagram? Find as many things as you can, including sides, angles and triangles. (Really, go take a look. We'll wait for you.)

There are many congruent things to find. Here is an incomplete list:

- AD = BC
- angle DEA = angle CEB
- angle D = angle C
- DB = CA

There are things you might suspect are congruent but can't be sure of yet. For instance, it certainly *looks* as though the small triangles on the left and right sides (ADE and BCE) are perfect, mirror-image copies of each other. But to be sure, we'll need to prove it.

This is the sort of problem I would open class with if I wanted to study a proof. The diagram and given information are just lifted directly from the upcoming proof. It's a preview of everything that will be developed further in the proof.

I made sure this problem had a *non-specific goal*. I didn't ask you to prove that AD and BC were congruent. I didn't ask you to find *all* the congruent angles. I asked you to find *as many congruencies as you could find*. Whether you found one, two or seven, as long as you were thinking then you were doing the right thing.

Very specific questions get us thinking about finding a specific answer. Like a dog given a familiar scent, we eagerly pursue a solution. But what happens if we don't want to send students off on a chase for an answer? What if instead we want students to explore the territory, getting used to the terrain?

Sweller and Levine identified "goal-free" problems as a type of question that fails to trigger the answer-chasing response.[70] These problems aren't entirely "free" of goals, but the goals are far less specific: "Figure out as many things as you can"; "Find angle values in the diagram"; "List as many congruencies as possible." They found (and others have confirmed)[71] that non-specific requests

---

70. Sweller, J., & Levine, M. (1982) "Effects of goal specificity on means-ends analysis and learning," *Journal of Experimental Psychology: Learning, Memory, and Cognition*, 8, 463–474.
71. Vollmeyer, R., Burns, B. D., & Holyoak, K. J. (1996) "The impact of goal specificity on strategy use and the acquisition of problem structure," *Cognitive Science*, 20 (1), 75–100.

don't trigger these unproductive, answer-chasing strategies. How could they? There is no specific request to chase. Instead, students are called to distribute their attention across the diagram, noticing many things.[72]

Before I introduce a proof, I often start with a goal-free problem. I'll ask students to figure out as much as they can on their own. Then, on the board, I make a list of things that are true about the diagram. I ask students to share what they've found and point out important things that students may not have mentioned. (Other times, I just make the list on my own.)

I think this technique can work for areas of mathematics besides geometry. For instance, I recently looked at lecture notes for an upper-level number theory course. In the second lecture the class studied a proof that began with this: "Prove that if a and m share no factors, and b and m share no factors, that ab shares no factors with m." To prepare students to study this proof, you might present a non-specific problem that goes like this:

"Neither a nor b *share any factors with* m.*"*

Figure out as many things additional things as you can about a, b, *or* m.

These goal-free problems can also serve as a checkpoint before entering the proof. Suppose that students are not able to understand the goal-free question, or they are not able to derive anything useful from the set-up. Is it really worth taking such a group of students into the proof? This may be a sign that class time would be better spent reviewing crucial ideas or learning more about ideas related to the proof.

Once the class has listed everything we'll need for the proof to come, we move on.

---

72. Goal-free problems are very similar to what other math educators call "open-ended" problems. For more, see the Further Reading section.

PREVIEW THE STRUCTURE

Remember: ABC and BAD are congruent. What about those "ears" on the sides, triangles AED and BEC? Are they guaranteed to be perfect copies as well?

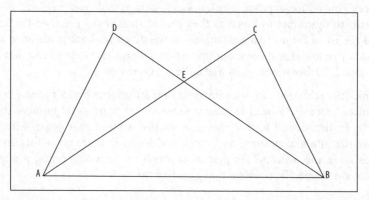

This is the question that is posed by the proof. The answer is "yes!" The proof explains why. Here is what the proof looks like, in the "two-column" format that is standard in many American schools.

Given: Δ *ABC* ≅ Δ *BAD*
Prove: Δ *AED* ≅ Δ *BEC*

Statement	Reason
Δ *ABC* ≅ Δ *BAD*	Given
∠*D* ≅ ∠*C*	Corresponding Parts of Congruent Triangles are Congruent (CPCTC)
$\overline{AD}$ ≅ $\overline{BC}$	Corresponding Parts of Congruent Triangles are Congruent (CPCTC)
∠ *DEA* ≅ ∠ *CEB*	Vertical angles are congruent
Δ *AED* ≅ Δ *BEC*	AAS

This is a lot for students to take in at first, even if they understand the underlying geometry. So at first, I don't show the proof to students.

Taking a page out of Mayer and Catrambone's research (Chapter 7), I highlight the structure of the proof for my students *before* showing it. "In just a moment I'm going to show you a proof that goes with this diagram. It's going to tell us that the overlapping triangles are congruent and challenge us to prove that these other triangles are congruent as well. Like every proof when two triangles are congruent, it's going to happen in three stages." On the board, I write a diagram sketching out the plan of the proof:

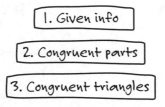

"We'll start by restating the given info. Then, we're going to use that starting info to look for parts that are congruent. This might take a bit of searching, but we want to keep in mind which triangles we're aiming to prove congruent. Then, once we have all the ingredients, we'll state our conclusion and explain which triangle theorem justifies it."

"Now let's look at the actual proof," I'll say.

I THINK ALOUD, YOU ANALYZE

If I were teaching a procedure, at this point I would reveal the example and walk away. When students can learn from reading the example, I tend to follow the pattern of worked example research and let students read it on their own. They get a quiet moment to analyze the solution and explain it to themselves, which is also a chance to get used to reading a piece of mathematics.

I don't have that option with proof. First, a lot of students will have trouble making heads or tails of it on their own. There's a lot of dense writing! Second, I want to show the process of creating a proof, not just the result. Even if they can follow the proof as written, its source may appear mysterious, as if it burst out of my skull fully formed. To produce proofs all on their own, students need an explanation of how they could have come up with it on their own.

I start thinking aloud: "I knew the given info was that these overlapping triangles were congruent. I did what we did at the start of class – I looked for as many congruent pieces in the diagram as I could find. We found congruent sides and congruent angles." I begin to highlight and annotate the diagram on the board (usually using a document camera). I use colors to draw connections between the diagram and the words in the proof, and I also try to highlight the steps where the actual thinking is happening:

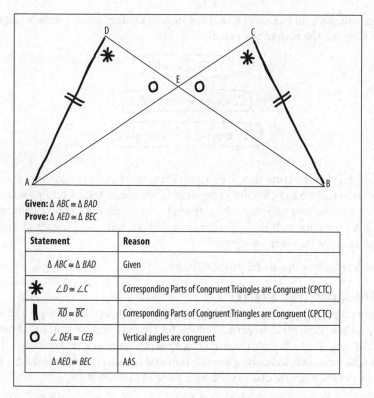

Given: Δ *ABC* ≅ Δ *BAD*
Prove: Δ *AED* ≅ Δ *BEC*

Statement	Reason
Δ *ABC* ≅ Δ *BAD*	Given
✱ ∠*D* ≅ ∠*C*	Corresponding Parts of Congruent Triangles are Congruent (CPCTC)
❙ $\overline{AD}$ ≅ $\overline{BC}$	Corresponding Parts of Congruent Triangles are Congruent (CPCTC)
O ∠ *DEA* ≅ *CEB*	Vertical angles are congruent
Δ *AED* ≅ *BEC*	AAS

I continue to explain not just the steps, but the thought process. "There were more pairs of congruent parts that we came up with at the start of class. But I knew that we were trying to prove the triangles on the sides are congruent. Angles like these on the bottom (BAD and ABC) are congruent, but I don't think they'd be as useful – the most useful things are sides or angles that are *part of* the triangles we're trying to prove congruent."

"I noticed that I had two pairs of angles and one pair of sides that are congruent. That's enough to prove the triangles congruent, so I knew I was done."

This sort of thinking aloud is called "modeling." (It is also called a "think-aloud.") Its use for teaching advanced problem solving was pioneered by mathematics education researcher Alan Schoenfeld.[73] Modeling has also been studied in the context of teaching students to solve more conventional problems. Studies often

73. Schoenfeld, A. H. (1992) "Learning to think mathematically: Problem solving, metacognition, and sense making in mathematics," in Grouws, D. A. (ed.) *Handbook of Research on Mathematics Teaching and Learning*. Macmillan.

find no difference in learning between students who learn via worked examples and those who learn from an instructor modeling a procedure.[74]

It would have been very difficult to represent my thinking in the worked example itself. How would I write an example that shows that I considered using the bottom angles, but ultimately decided not to? Modeling, or thinking aloud, was the way to go. But modeling creates two instructional dilemmas:

1. The information I've shared about my thought process is not all in the diagram. I try to draw as much as I can on the board, but some things are difficult to capture in annotation.

2. Since I've provided the bulk of the explanation, it no longer makes sense for me to ask students to explain each step of the proof as I usually do as part of my worked example routine.

My approach to addressing both these concerns at once is to ask students to summarize ideas that I just modeled. This plays roughly the same role as the self-explanation prompts that I shared earlier in the book. Rather than reading a worked example, students have just heard me talk aloud about creating a proof. Many students will naturally ask themselves questions to check their own understanding. Other students will not. Prompting students to analyze and summarize the think-aloud can help make sure they've thought deeply about it.

I'll take a copy of the proof we've been discussing and hand a copy of it to each student. "Take a few minutes and annotate the diagram with any congruent parts," I'll say. "Then, answer the questions on the page." These questions ask students to remember key elements of the process I modeled. For the proof above, analysis questions could be:

How could we know that the top angles in the diagram (C and D) are congruent?

Why might angles D and C be more useful to this proof than angles DAB and CBA?

These types of questions will hopefully push students towards explaining the proof more carefully to themselves, or else realizing they need help in better understanding it. Indeed, there is research finding that asking students to self-explain (as well as preparing students to self-explain through analysis of excellent explanations) helps students understand complex proofs.[75]

---

74. Hoogerheide, V., Loyens, S. M., & Van Gog, T. (2014) "Comparing the effects of worked examples and modeling examples on learning," *Computers in Human Behavior*, 41, 80–91.

75. Hodds, M., Alcock, L., & Inglis, M. (2014) "Self-explanation training improves proof comprehension," *Journal for Research in Mathematics Education*, 45 (1), 62–101.

LOTS OF WHOLE-TASK PRACTICE

At the start of class I gave my students a "goal-free" problem that helped them to notice and remember key info for understanding the proof. Students have now had a chance to analyze the proof and explain important elements of it. It's time to ask them to apply the solution to new cases.

I am a heavy user of completion problems for practicing writing proofs. It's easy to create completion problems by removing a step from the finished product. As with example-problem pairs, I try to change just one thing between the example we've just studied and the proof to complete – in this case, a different reason justifies why the triangles are congruent in the final step:

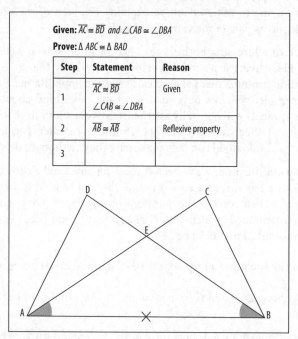

I'll use completion problems *a lot* while teaching proof. Compared to my teaching of other topics, a lot more time is spent using these sorts of half-example/half-problem forms of practice.

In Chapter 5 I borrowed the phrase "whole-task practice" from researchers. These forms of practice let students focus on parts of a skill while maintaining the overall setting of the whole skill. Completion problems are like that – they allow students to focus their attention on just one part of a proof *in* a mostly complete proof.

Proofs are complex beasts with many moving parts. This is why whole-task practice is more necessary, but it also means there are many more ways to generate practice of this kind.

Mathematics educators Michelle Cirillo and Patricio Herbst have a long, rich list of meaningful ways that students can practice geometry proof.[76] Their article was a real revelation to me – I'd never considered so many different ways of practicing proof! – but their formula for generating these practice formats is relatively simple: take every element that goes into writing a proof and knock it (and only it!) out of the proof, leaving it for students to complete. Their creative ideas include:

Draw the diagram: Provide students with a "Given" and "Prove" statement and ask them to generate a diagram.

Draw a diagram that could be used to prove the following:

Given: Parallelogram *PQRS* where *T* is the midpoint of $\overline{PQ}$ and *V* is the midpoint of $\overline{SR}$

Prove: $\overline{ST} \cong \overline{QV}$

Missing "Given": Provide students with a mostly full proof and ask them to reason out what the given information was.

What given information could be used to complete this proof?

Step	Statement	Reason
1	???	Given
2	$\overline{AD} \cong \overline{DC}$	A midpoint divides a segment into two congruent segments
3	$\overline{BD} \cong \overline{BD}$	Reflexive property
4	$\triangle ABD \cong \triangle CBD$	SSS

---

76. Cirillo, M., & Herbst, P. G. (2012) "Moving toward more authentic proof practices in geometry," *The Mathematics Educator*, 21 (2).

Missing "Prove": Provide students with a diagram and given information and ask them to list possible "Prove" statements that a proof could end with. This has some similarities to the goal-free problems that we started with:

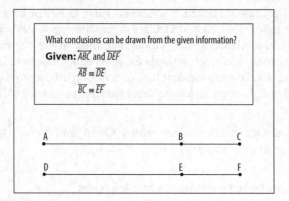

Mistake analysis: Find an error in a mostly correct proof:

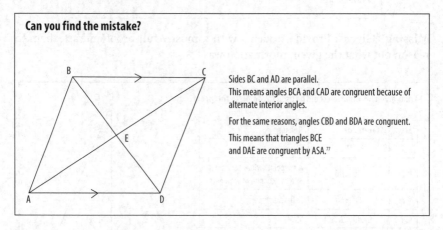

Another excellent resource for proof practice is the website DeltaMath. Their website contains even more whole-task practice formats. Here are two more to add to the growing list:

---

77. This proof is presented in "paragraph" form rather than in the two-column format. I will usually teach several formats for writing geometry proofs, including flowcharts. There are many good examples of flowchart proof in the textbook *Discovering Geometry* (Key Curriculum Press), written by Michael Serra.

Missing reasons: All the steps of the proof are given, but students are asked to provide just the reasons justifying those steps:

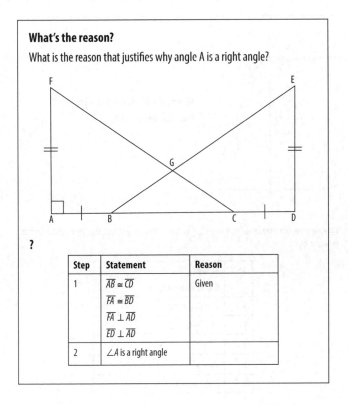

What's the reason?

What is the reason that justifies why angle A is a right angle?

Step	Statement	Reason
1	$\overline{AB} \cong \overline{CD}$	Given
	$\overline{FA} \cong \overline{BD}$	
	$\overline{FA} \perp \overline{AD}$	
	$\overline{ED} \perp \overline{AD}$	
2	$\angle A$ is a right angle	

Reorder the steps: All the steps of the proof are given, but in the wrong order. Students are asked to arrange the steps in a logical sequence:

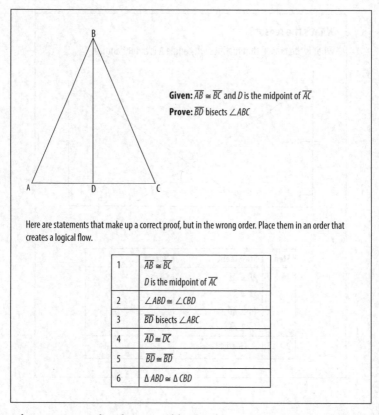

Given: $\overline{AB} \cong \overline{BC}$ and D is the midpoint of $\overline{AC}$
Prove: $\overline{BD}$ bisects $\angle ABC$

Here are statements that make up a correct proof, but in the wrong order. Place them in an order that creates a logical flow.

1	$\overline{AB} \cong \overline{BC}$
	D is the midpoint of $\overline{AC}$
2	$\angle ABD \cong \angle CBD$
3	$\overline{BD}$ bisects $\angle ABC$
4	$\overline{AD} \cong \overline{DC}$
5	$\overline{BD} \cong \overline{BD}$
6	$\triangle ABD \cong \triangle CBD$

As students practice they become able to take on more and more of the proof writing. Eventually, it's time for students to write their own proofs from scratch. To help this transition to more independence, I sometimes give students a blank page containing *only* the high-level structure of a proof (like the one I shared earlier). Students can fill in the details on their own:

Write a proof with statements and reasons

1. State given information:
2. Find congruent parts:
3. Conclude that two triangles are congruent:

Only after students are growing confident with these sorts of practice formats will I ask them to write their own proofs from scratch.

It's true this process does take a lot of time. I rarely practice proof in all these many ways. My own proof unit is only a few weeks long, and it follows a lot of careful thinking and practice about congruence that doesn't use all this fancy language. But there comes a time when my class has all the pieces ready, and just needs to practice putting them together using precise language and careful logical ordering. That's when I begin teaching and practicing formal proof in the ways I detailed above. I'll continue practicing this formal style of proof throughout the year, even after we turn to other topics.

This all goes to show that worked examples can be used to teach some of the trickiest mathematical skills. But it's not the only way I know that studying examples can help a student get better at proof.

The toughest geometry proofs for me involve auxiliary lines and transformations. Experts in this craft can contort the starting diagram in all sorts of interesting ways. They add a line here, draw a perpendicular there, rotate this bit that way and then – BAM! – all of a sudden there is an entirely new structure to the diagram, seemingly plucked out of thin air. And yet it plays by all the rules –

no added assumptions. Do it right, and what you add to the diagram simply reveals connections between angles and lines that were already there waiting to be discovered. "Best Witchcraft is Geometry," starts an Emily Dickinson poem. I know what she means.

For years I hit my head against the wall trying to get better at this type of problem. I would work for days on a single problem. The problems clearly called for creativity, but it was a creativity I didn't seem to have in me. I was convinced that the key was persistence. What I needed to do was stick with a problem long enough to have a breakthrough. Wasn't solving problems the only way to make progress?

Creativity clearly is the key to these problems, but that doesn't mean knowledge doesn't help. My first breakthrough was when I realized that other people simply knew more than me. I got myself an advanced geometry book and started reading the theorems. It turned out there were a lot of useful ones that I'd never even heard of. I also started to look more carefully at the solutions that others created for the problems. I realized that if I wanted to be initiated into the craft of advanced geometry, there was no royal road: I'd have to study solutions.

Studying solutions is not enough; anyone can tell you that. But I remember my first breakthrough. I was reading solutions to a problem I had gotten stuck on, and I came across one that I thought was truly beautiful. It concerned a triangle with all sorts of complicated given information that had been divided into two smaller triangles:

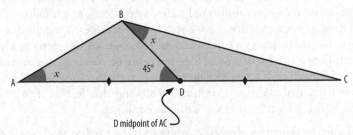

The solution I read used a truly beautiful idea that never would have occurred to me. It saw this triangle as secretly inscribed in a circle:

114

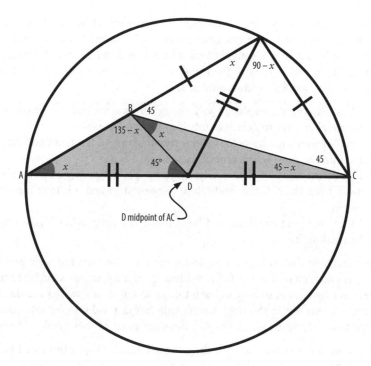

This turned out to be the key insight that helped them solve the problem. I was blown away.

I realized that this only worked because the long side of the triangle was split in half. This gave me something like a little hint to place into my toolkit: *if a triangle is divided so that several lengths radiate from some central point, it might be useful to see the diagram as inscribed in a circle.*

I also remember the first time I solved a challenging problem using this idea. It felt so wonderful to have made a bit of progress on something that had given me so much frustration.

On my desk now is a great book titled *Challenging Problems in Geometry.* The book is split into three parts: "Problems," "Hints" and "Solutions." The "Solutions" section is the longest. What I'm loving is trying a problem just up to the exact moment that it stops being enjoyable. Then I flip towards the solutions in the back. Often the book presents several solutions, which are fun to compare. (It's amazing how many ways in mathematics there are to arrive at the same result.)

This is new territory for me. I don't have an experienced teacher to guide me through these solutions in a systematic way. I *wish* somebody could hand me practice that let me focus on precisely what it is I need to improve at. Unlike my students, I'm on my own. Still, I'm roughly following the sequence of learning that I have designed for my own students:

- I first explore the problem well enough to understand the situation thoroughly. I try to derive as much as I can on my own.
- I look towards the hints to preview the structure of the proof and clue me into the most important ideas.
- I study the solution(s) carefully. I try to explain it on my own. I walk away from the solution and try to recreate it myself. I'll take a note or two.
- I'll try the next problem, and hope that I can apply what I have just learned to this new case.

It's that last step that is hardest to do on my own, because the next problem rarely gives me a chance to use the new ideas from the previous solution. This is one reason why it takes so long to learn things on our own – we have to *find* our own applications out in the wild. I can't help but feel jealousy for my students at times, that they have teachers to give them the practice they need to improve.

I'm enjoying the problems and reading the solutions. Slowly, but steadily, I'm also getting better at the problems. Mathematics will never be easy, but studying other people's solutions helps.

IN SHORT

- Worked examples can be used to help teach complex and creative mathematics. The key challenge is uncovering the process of creating the final product, rather than just sharing the ideal result.
- I use **goal-free problems** to help prepare students for the proof (and assess whether they're ready for it). I then **preview the structure** of the proof for students. Once the proof is revealed, I **think-aloud** about a process one could use to create such a proof. Students answer **analysis questions** about this modeling, and then apply what they've seen to a new, similar proof situation.
- The complexity of proof makes **whole-task practice** formats especially useful. There are many excellent ways to focus students' attention on the many specific pieces of writing a proof using completion problems.

AFTERWORD: THE BIG IDEAS OF TEACHING WITH EXAMPLES

Looking back on this book, I was surprised to notice several ideas that repeat themselves across chapters. As I see it, here are those big ideas.

For the purpose of learning, it doesn't matter who comes up with an idea on their own. What matters is thinking deeply about ideas, wherever they come from. Because of this we should rethink a value system that praises problem solving which thinks of studying solutions as "giving up" (Preface). Likewise, we shouldn't prioritize inquiry over direct instruction in our classrooms *as long as* we guarantee that students are thinking deeply about the ideas we share with them (Chapter 1). Since the ultimate source of an explanation is less important than how students interact with it, as teachers we might choose to explain a worked example or not, depending on the situation (Chapters 3 and 4). When it comes to proof, it may be important to model the creation process so that students can analyze and explain it (Chapter 8).

Nothing works unless students are actively thinking. A person can solve a problem without really thinking about the solution (Chapter 1). Notes are only useful to the extent that taking them causes deep thought (Chapter 4). Feedback is often useless because it fails to get students thinking – it usually just explains why a student did or did not answer a question correctly (Chapter 6). We should plan on provoking this deeper sort of engagement from students. A crucial part of the planning is the art of design, which is the art of creating materials that let students focus on what is important (Chapter 7).

There is a type of practice that is undervalued in education: whole-task practice, which lets students focus on specific steps while preserving the overall context of the skill. I use this sort of practice to help students move from examples to independent problem solving (Chapter 5). This is something I draw on heavily while teaching proof (Chapter 8). You could even make the case that revision – a key part of how I give feedback – also falls under this umbrella (Chapter 6). Especially as skills grow more complex, this sort of practice is increasingly useful.

The same teaching principles look different in different contexts. When it comes to teaching procedures, I usually present a worked example and let students explain it themselves (Chapter 3). But with teaching proofs, I don't do this (Chapter 8). We shouldn't expect teaching to look the same in every classroom, even if it's built on the same underlying educational ideas.

Research and teachers need each other. You can't simply take the ideas of research and bring them into the classroom. One way of putting this is that teaching cannot really be *based* in evidence, even if it is *informed* by it (Chapters 3 and 4). We teachers need to be flexible in how we use what we read about. You can see this flexibility in action when you look at topics that are more difficult to teach, such as proof (Chapter 8). It would be good for education if researchers and teachers were in much closer conversation with each other.

FURTHER READING

PREFACE
Two cultures of mathematics

Mathematician Tim Gowers describes a cultural divide among research mathematicians, between those who are oriented towards solving problems and those who seek to develop theories:

Gowers, W. T. (2000) "The two cultures of mathematics," in Arnold, V. et al. (eds.) *Mathematics: Frontiers and Perspectives*, 65–78. American Mathematical Society.

I think this is related to my point in the Preface, though in the case of research mathematics the situation is reversed: what's dominant is the culture of theoretical understanding and problem solving sometimes takes a backseat. I developed some of my thoughts in the Preface further in a blog post:

Pershan, M. (2018) "I don't focus my classroom on solving problems," *Teaching With Problems:* https://problemproblems.wordpress.com/2018/08/22/a-culture-of-understanding/

INTRODUCTION & CHAPTER 1
Reviews of the worked example literature

A single study isn't worth very much. When we talk about what "evidence" or "the research" supports, the evidence has to come from many sources – otherwise, its findings can only be suggestive.

In the body of the text, I cite many individual studies. I took care not to "cherry pick" papers that narrowly support my point (something that bugs me to no end when I read writing about teaching). What I drew from, mostly, were reviews of the worked example literature that bring together and summarize many studies. One of the most important of these literature reviews is:

Atkinson, R. K., Derry, S. J., Renkl, A., & Wortham, D. (2000) "Learning from examples: Instructional principles from the worked examples research," *Review of Educational Research*, 70 (2), 181–214.

There are other, more recent reviews of the worked example literature. This very recent article isn't a review of the literature, but it does describe many of the ways worked example research has developed in the 20 years since Atkinson et al.'s review:

> Scheiter, K. (2020) "Embracing complexity in research on learning from examples and from problem solving," *Applied Cognitive Psychology*, 34 (4), 906–911.

Worked example research these days increasingly looks at learning that is a bit messier (like proof), thinks about things like motivation, and takes an interest in classroom research.

This recent review is good, but somewhat difficult to access (it's a book chapter):

> Gog, T. V., Rummel, N., & Renkl, A. (2019) "Learning how to solve problems by studying examples," in Dunlosky, J. & Rawson, K. A. (eds.), *The Cambridge Handbook of Cognition and Education*, 183–208. Cambridge University Press.

There are also useful guides for practitioners that have collected this research and digested it into teaching ideas. This one has been helpful to me, and can be found for free online:

> Woodward, J., Beckmann, S., Driscoll, M., Franke, M., Herzig, P., Jitendra, A., Koedinger, K. R., & Ogbuehi, P. (2012) *Improving Mathematical Problem Solving in Grades 4 Through 8*. Institute of Education Sciences.

How Americans teach

The TIMSS video study collected footage from math and science classrooms in the US, Germany and Japan. In Chapter 1 I cited a paper from that study that found there are differences between how subjects are taught in these different countries. For more on these differences, check out *The Teaching Gap*:

> Stigler, J. W., & Hiebert, J. (2009) *The Teaching Gap: Best ideas from the world's teachers for improving education in the classroom*. Simon & Schuster.

Algebra/Math by Example and design-based research

The materials produced by this project were so influential to my understanding of worked examples. The project has produced both robust empirical research and helpful guides for practitioners:

McGinn, K. M., Lange, K. E., & Booth, J. L. (2015) "A worked example for creating worked examples," *Mathematics Teaching in the Middle School*, 21 (1), 26–33.

Booth, J. L., Lange, K. E., Koedinger, K. R., & Newton, K. J. (2013) "Using example problems to improve student learning in algebra: Differentiating between correct and incorrect examples," *Learning and Instruction*, 25, 24–34.

In the text, I express my admiration for the partnership between researchers and a district that produced the Algebra by Example project. The project is an effort by the SERP Institute, which specializes in incubating these sorts of partnerships. I really admire these "Research Practitioner Partnerships," and I'd love to see them become more widespread.

CHAPTER 2
Behaviorism and the emergence of cognitive science

The emergence of cognitive science is such an interesting story. Dan Willingham's introductory textbook doesn't overlap much with this book, but it does contain a very clear account of the scientific and philosophical environment in which cognitive science emerged:

Willingham, D. T., & Riener, C. (2019) *Cognition: The thinking animal*. Cambridge University Press.

For a readable account from a researcher who was there at the start, check out:

Miller, G. A. (2003) "The cognitive revolution: a historical perspective," *Trends in Cognitive Sciences*, 7 (3), 141–144.

Miller argues that there were six fields involved in this milieu: psychology, linguistics, neuroscience, computer science, anthropology and philosophy.

It's worth noting that Herb Simon, one of the leading researchers in the emergence of cognitive science (he eventually won a Nobel Prize in economics), was also there at the start of worked example research:

Zhu, X., & Simon, H. A. (1987) "Learning mathematics from examples and by doing," *Cognition and Instruction*, 4 (3), 137–166.

Simon, H. A. (1998) "What we know about learning," *Journal of Engineering Education*, 87 (4), 343–348.

His story is fascinating. He began by trying to understand how institutions (such as a business or team) learn and solve problems. To test his ideas, he got involved in computer simulation and helped to create the field of artificial intelligence and machine learning. And then he performed one of the first experiments that supports the efficacy of learning from examples.

He won the Nobel Prize for his foundational work in behavioral economics, by the way.

John Sweller and cognitive load theory

John Sweller's research is all over this book. He, more than anyone else, is responsible for launching research into worked examples. Thanks to widespread interest among educators in him there are now many readable introductions to his work.

A great place to start is Sweller's own account of his career and the development of his "cognitive load theory":

Sweller, J. (2016) "Story of a research program," *Education Review*, 23.

Cognitive load theory influenced a lot of this book (especially Chapters 2 and 7). I wrote an online essay describing the development of cognitive load theory, from the perspective of the choices and trade-offs that go into any scientific theory:

Pershan, M. (2016) "Not a theory of everything: On cognitive load theory and the complexity of learning," https://cognitiveloadtheory. wordpress.com

---

CHAPTER 3
Can teaching be evidence-based?

Some scholars have critiqued the notion of "best practices" in teaching. Their argument is that it's challenging to summarize good teaching through a single best practice, since context is so important for whether a practice works or not. For a deep-dive into this concept, check out this book (especially the opening chapters):

Lefstein, A., & Snell, J. (2013). *Better Than Best Practice: Developing teaching and learning through dialogue*. Routledge.

The importance of self-explanation

For a thorough discussion of self-explanation, check out Chapter 5 of Craig Barton's excellent book *How I Wish I'd Taught Maths*:

Barton, C. (2018) *How I Wish I'd Taught Maths: Lessons learned from research, conversations with experts, and 12 years of mistakes.* John Catt Educational.

Really, it's worth picking up Craig's book in any event. He has thoughtfully digested an enormous amount of research and writes compellingly about how it has impacted his teaching.

CHAPTER 4

Associating strategies with (fictional) students

How names interact with worked examples is an active area of research. For example, a very recent paper tested whether names matter in the context of "case comparisons" that call on students to compare two different worked-out approaches. This study found no negative effect to associating strategies with names in this context.

Loehr, A., Rittle-Johnson, B., Durkin, K., & Star, J. R. (2020) "Does calling it 'Morgan's way' reduce student learning? Evaluating the effect of person-presentation during comparison and discussion of worked examples in mathematics classrooms," *Applied Cognitive Psychology*, 34 (4), 825–836.

CHAPTER 5

Whole-task practice and complex learning

The notion of "whole-task" practice was something I first encountered in Paul Kirschner and Jeroen van Merriënboer's book, *Ten Steps to Complex Learning*:

Van Merriënboer, J. J., & Kirschner, P. A. (2017) *Ten Steps to Complex Learning: A systematic approach to four-component instructional design.* Routledge.

They present an instructional model that has complex, professional training in mind. In these areas of teaching, there is often a large gap between instructional settings and real-world applications. They don't apply this model to academic contexts that are more typical of k-12 settings, but it still makes for an interesting read.

The distinction between whole-task and part-task practice goes back at least over a century in psychological research. Many researchers point to Lottie Steffens' studies on poetry memorization as the beginning of this area of research. I came across references to Steffens' work in several early papers, for example:

McGeoch, G. O. (1932) "A revaluation of the whole-part problem in learning," *The Journal of Educational Research*, 26 (1), 1–5.

Steffens was interested in whether it was more efficient for students to memorize the entire poem at once or in parts. Today, one is most likely to come across the whole-task/part-task distinction in athletic coaching or physical rehabilitation, fields that focus on the teaching of various physical movements.

CHAPTER 6
Why is feedback research so hard?

This is a question that I was a bit obsessed with for several years. My perspective is spread out over several pieces I wrote online, all of which can be found here:

Pershan, M. (2019) "Excerpts from my outbox: Where are all the good readings about feedback," *Teaching With Problems:* https://problemproblems.wordpress.com/category/feedback/

My approach to feedback research is a critical one. I don't attempt to synthesize the various findings into a single system. Instead, my approach in this book was to reduce the lessons of research into a simple insight – that feedback is either teaching or motivation and nothing else.

For an extremely thoughtful and thorough attempt to systematize the feedback literature, you can't do better than Harry Fletcher-Wood's book:

Fletcher-Wood, H. (2018) *Responsive Teaching: Cognitive science and formative assessment in practice.* Routledge.

You can see an early version of Chapter 8 appear as a vignette in Harry's book.

CHAPTER 7
Well-designed materials

There are several workbooks and texts whose design I admire. A favorite is the *Transition to Algebra* series, for helping middle-school students begin their work in algebra:

> Mark, J., Goldenberg, E. P., Fries, M., Kang, J. M., & Cordner, T. (2014) *Transition to Algebra*. Heinemann.

The *Math in Focus* workbooks (Grades K–8) contain cleanly written worked examples that are integrated tightly with practice:

> Gan, K. S., & Ramakrishnan, C. (2009) *Math in Focus: Singapore Math*. Houghton Mifflin School.

Illustrative Mathematics is a free, open curriculum for Grades 6–12 (K–5 is in development). Especially in their units on solving equations they use well-designed worked examples, completion problems and case comparisons. A good example comes in the Grade 8, Unit 4 materials:

> https://im.kendallhunt.com/MS/students/3/4/4/index.html

I have often mentioned the *Algebra by Example* project throughout this book. Their materials for younger students can be found here:

> https://www.serpinstitute.org/math-by-example

For worked examples of challenging mathematics, a wonderful resource is the Shell Center's *Mathematics Assessment Project*:

> https://www.map.mathshell.org/

CHAPTER 8
Goal-free and open-ended problems

Goal-free problems are useful for introducing challenges. I also find them useful as short pre-assessments, since more students are able to answer them before I've taught the class anything.

Goal-free problems were studied by Sweller and incorporated into his cognitive load theory. Any introduction to cognitive load theory will explain their role in that theory.

My favorite source of open-ended problems are the *Good Questions* books by Marian Small and Amy Lin. I like keeping these books within reach, since they are full of interesting and useful questions:

Small, M. (2012) *Good Questions: Great ways to differentiate mathematics instruction.* Teachers College Press.

Small, M., & Lin, A. (2010) *More Good Questions: Great ways to differentiate secondary mathematics instruction.* Teachers College Press.

Neither of these authors think that open-ended questions should make up all, or even most, of what a student encounters. But they make a nice addition to the mix.

Michelle Cirilo's writing on proof

Geometry proof is not something that very many people study or write about. Unlike algebra, it's not deemed a major priority for students. Schools focus resources and attention on algebra, which is crucial for careers in a way that proof is not.

Michelle Cirillo wrote a paper that I cited in Chapter 8. She has written many very practical articles on teaching proof:

Cirillo, M. (2009) "Ten things to consider when teaching proof," *The Mathematics Teacher*, 103 (4), 250–257.

Cirillo, M., & Hummer, J. (2019) "Addressing misconceptions in secondary geometry proof," *The Mathematics Teacher*, 112 (6), 410–417.

Cirillo, M., & Herbst, P. G. (2012) "Moving toward more authentic proof practices in geometry," *The Mathematics Educator*, 21 (2).

I find her writing very useful in my teaching of proof.